THE

ABOLITIONIST
MOVEMENT

ENDING SLAVERY

REFORM MOVEMENTS
IN AMERICAN
HISTORY

THE

ABOLITIONIST
MOVEMENT

ENDING SLAVERY

Tim McNeese

CHELSEA HOUSE
PUBLISHERS
An imprint of Infobase Publishing

The Abolitionist Movement: Ending Slavery

Copyright © 2008 by Infobase Publishing

Chelsea House
An imprint of Infobase Publishing
132 West 31st Street
New York NY 10001

Library of Congress Cataloging-in-Publication Data
McNeese, Tim.
  The abolitionist movement : ending slavery / Tim McNeese.
    p. cm. — (Reform movements in American history)
  Includes bibliographical references and index.
  ISBN-13: 978-0-7910-9502-7 (hardcover)
  ISBN-10: 0-7910-9502-9 (hardcover)
  1. Antislavery movements—United States—History—19th century—Juvenile literature. 2. Abolitionists—United States—History—19th century—Juvenile literature. 3. Slavery—United States—History—19th century—Juvenile literature. I. Title.
  E449.M173 2007
  973.7'114--dc22
                        2007014766

Chelsea House books are available at special discounts when purchased in bulk quantities for businesses, associations, institutions, or sales promotions. Please call our Special Sales Department in New York at (212) 967-8800 or (800) 322-8755.

You can find Chelsea House on the World Wide Web at http://www.chelseahouse.com

Series design by Kerry Casey
Cover design by Ben Peterson

Printed in the United States of America

Bang FOF 10 9 8 7 6 5 4 3 2 1

This book is printed on acid-free paper.

All links and Web addresses were checked and verified to be correct at the time of publication. Because of the dynamic nature of the Web, some addresses and links may have changed since publication and may no longer be valid.

CONTENTS

1

John Brown's Crusade

In the predawn darkness of October 17, 1859, a train conductor ordered a railroad telegrapher to send a desperate message down the line. Earlier that morning, his train, a passenger line moving east from Virginia and bound for Baltimore, Maryland, had been stopped by a small band of armed men. The incident had taken place at Monocacy, Maryland, across the river from a small town situated at the vee formed by the flow of the Shenandoah River into the greatest of Virginia's rivers, the Potomac. The conductor's message was clear and straight to the point: "My train eastbound was stopped at Harpers Ferry this morning about 1:30 by armed abolitionists."[1]

Abolitionists—those opposed to the existence of slavery and who demanded its immediate eradication—had stopped a train in western Virginia. With the nightriders described as abolitionists in his alarm, the train conductor would certainly not be ignored. In 1859, such men and women were considered radicals and extremists, the mid-nineteenth-century version of homegrown American terrorists. They were a motley group, small in number, and included both whites and blacks. They were led by a fiery-eyed zealot whose long gray beard may have made him look older than his age. His name was well known throughout the United States. He was an abolitionist who justified violence and murder as a means to end an institution he considered a work of Satan and his legions. He was "Old Brown of Osawatomie"—John Brown.

CREATION OF A JOSHUA

John Brown had managed to remain a virtual unknown on the stage of American history for the first 50 years of his life. Born in Connecticut, he came into the world with the new century in 1800. He grew up on the Ohio frontier, where he was "taught in local schools to resent compulsory education and by his parents to revere the Bible and hate slavery."[2] During the War of 1812, while still a youth, he herded cattle for General William Hull's army. As a young adult, he worked in his father's tannery. Brown married, first at 20 years of age. After his wife, Dianthe, died in childbirth with their seventh child in 1832, Brown remarried three years later to a 16-year-old girl named Mary. He was the father of 20 children. He spent decades attempting to make a success of farming but failed. He tried a variety of business ventures that included working as a tanner, a land speculator, a shepherd, and a wool merchant; each of those endeavors also failed. Through these years, he became "too much a visionary, not enough a businessman."[3]

Abolitionism came simply to Brown. After he watched "a white man beating a slave boy with a shovel,"[4] he began to hate slavery. (Perhaps ironically, though, Brown was known to lash his own children if they told white lies, did their chores too slowly, or committed any other infractions.) As his children grew up, they were constantly impressed by their father's dedication to racial equality and his affection for blacks. He attended churches where he and his family sat side by side with African Americans. A daughter, Ruth, remembered that her father asked her "how I would like to have some poor little black children that were slaves . . . come and live with us" and then asked "if I would be willing to divide my food and clothes with them."[5] Brown's fervor kicked into high gear in the fall of 1837, after an antislavery editor in Alton, Illinois, Elijah P. Lovejoy, was murdered by members of a white mob while he defended his printing press. When Brown attended a meeting in a Congregational church in Hudson, Ohio, and listened to the minister talk about the death of Lovejoy, Brown became convinced that he had to become an abolitionist. He stood up from his pew in the back of the church, raised his right hand, and swore an oath that he never turned away from: "Here, before God, in the presence of these witnesses, from this time, I consecrate my life to the destruction of slavery!"[6]

Brown's visions were focused on America's future, as well as its present and past. As an adult, he had come to despise slavery. So much in life had not gone his way. He struggled to make ends meet, and he found the world wearisome and a burden. He was a poor man and knew it. He developed a keen sense of what it was like to be looked down on and felt oppressed at every turn. In time, he came to identify with the plight of many blacks, in the belief that he shared their miseries. He began to associate with blacks socially and chose to live in a community of freed blacks for two years in North Elba, New York. Blacks became his obsession and their freedom his life's work. Brown became a militant abolitionist, one who not only opposed slavery intellectually and emotionally but also was prepared to do anything that would bring about freedom for all slaves held in the United States. He put his obsession into action and became a "conductor" on the Underground Railroad. He formed a self-protection league for free blacks. Brown's efforts were sustained by his reading of Scripture. He saw himself as a biblical Joshua, a warrior for God, intent on defeating his enemies. He was fiery, led by verses that gave him direction and the voice of a prophet. His favorite was from the New Testament, Hebrews 9:22: "Without the shedding of blood, there is no remission of sins."

John Brown, pictured here in 1857, believed that slavery was a sin against Christianity and devoted his life's work to bringing about its end. He was the first white abolitionist to advocate insurrection as a way to combat slavery and fought alongside his sons to make Kansas a free state.

By age 50, Brown had visions of bloodshed and slave revolts, which would require slaveholders to pay for their sins with their lives. Then, in the fall of 1855, he went to Kansas, where slavery was a contentious issue. The previous year, the U.S. Congress had passed a bill that not only created the Territory of Kansas but also opened it to slavery. Called the Kansas-Nebraska Act, this piece of legislation replaced an agreement congressmen had made more than 30 years earlier—the Missouri Compromise. Under that agreement, slavery had been banned from any future territory that bordered Missouri to the west and north. In the heat of the slavery issue and in the hands of another generation of American leaders, however, that decision was usurped and slavery given new possibilities in Kansas. However, Brown would not stand by and watch the advance of slavery.

Five of Brown's sons had already moved to Kansas, and once Brown joined them, the six men took matters into their own hands. With the future of Kansas undecided, supporters and opponents of slavery converged on the territory, ready to fight for their respective causes. The next year, after proslavery men attacked and burned the Free Soil town of Lawrence, Brown flew into a fury. We must "fight fire with fire!"[7] he declared. We must "strike terror in the hearts of the proslavery people."[8] Then he received word that a Northern abolitionist senator, Charles Sumner of Massachusetts, had been nearly beaten to death on May 22, 1856, by an angry congressman from South Carolina, Preston Brooks, for a speech he delivered in opposition to slavery. Brown went *crazy*, witnesses claimed, when he heard the news. "Something must be done to show these barbarians that we, too, have rights,"[9] he announced. He organized a volunteer militia of followers who lived near his Osawatomie River home and sought revenge. They found it when, on the night of May 24–25, Brown and six followers (four of whom were his own sons) raided the homes of a proslavery settlement near Pottawatomie Creek. Five unarmed men were dragged from their homes into the dark Kansas night, where Brown and his men "coolly split open their skulls with broadswords."[10] The antislavery men then removed their victims' entrails and scattered them across the ground. The name John Brown was soon on the lips of every Kansas resident, as well as those Americans who lived beyond the territory's borders. Old Brown of Osawatomie was a name both anxiously feared and violently despised. That fear notwithstanding, proslavery bands attacked and burned the Brown family homesteads in retaliation.

That fall, a wanted man with a price on his head, John Brown left Kansas and found his way to Ohio. During the years that followed, the territory still suffered from proslavery and antislavery violence, and he went to Kansas on two occasions. In May 1858, near the second anniversary of the Pottawatomie Massacre, a proslavery party rounded up nine Free Soilers in their homes, lined them up, formed a makeshift firing squad, and shot them. On one of his retaliatory raids, Brown and his followers went into Missouri, from where many of the proslavery men hailed, killed a slaveholder, and freed 11 slaves, as well as a good stock of horses, which Brown took north to Canada. Before the era of "Bleeding Kansas" came to an end in the late 1850s, approximately 200 lives would be lost, including that of one of Brown's sons, through vigilante attacks on both sides. In time, he began to develop a new plan of action in his campaign against slavery. He decided to instigate a slave uprising; one that might, once begun, extend across the South in great angry ripples, and tear down the institution that Brown hated so much.

Brown would not keep to himself his plan to bring about a wholesale uprising. He would need money, and he relied on six Northern men—a group later identified as the Secret Six—for support. In August 1859, just two months before his planned raid, Brown met with one of the most important and influential black abolitionist leaders in the country, Frederick Douglass, to declare his intentions. He wanted Douglass to join in the plan, but Douglass was unconvinced and refused to take part. The black leader told Brown his whole plan was nothing short of suicide. He did find support from another black leader, however. In April 1858, Brown visited the Canadian community of

St. Catharines, Ontario, just north of Buffalo, New York. The town was home to approximately 1,000 former slaves who had made their way to freedom after they escaped from the South. There, Brown met with Harriet Tubman, a former slave whose work as a conductor on the Underground Railroad of safe houses for escaped slaves was well known. Tubman had helped hundreds of slaves to escape along the Underground Railroad and had repeatedly risked her life each time she returned to the South. Brown greatly admired Tubman and called her "General Tubman." He told her of his plan to lead a massive slave revolt and asked her to join him. She agreed and promised to help raise support for the plan. (When the assault actually took place, Tubman was sick and unable to participate directly.)

RAID AT HARPERS FERRY

John Brown's plan was to launch an assault at Harpers Ferry, Virginia. (Today, Harpers Ferry is located in the state of West Virginia, which was not yet a separate state in 1859.) Harpers Ferry was a small village of 3,000 inhabitants, and "had been home to one of two national armories since George Washington's presidency."[11] Brown intended to steal a large number of government-owned weapons from the arsenal and arm slaves throughout the region of the Shenandoah, which would set off a massive slave revolt. He and the freed slaves would head for the nearby mountains and hide out, and they would free more slaves as they went along. At least, that was the plan.

Brown's preparations for his raid were certainly well organized and thoughtfully prepared, even if ultimately ill conceived. In May, he sent one of his followers, John E. Cook, to Harpers Ferry, Virginia, to take up residence. Cook was to become acquainted with the local countryside and the town's citizens. He was to make contact with as many

On October 16, 1859, John Brown and a group of 21 men seized the U.S. Armory at Harpers Ferry, Virginia, in the hopes of taking weapons and munitions, which they planned to use to help free the town's slaves. The shell of the arsenal is pictured in this photo from the 1890s, 30 years after it had been torched by the Union Army at the beginning of the Civil War.

local slaves as possible, quietly, in order not to be noticed. On July 1, under a fictitious name—Isaac Smith—Brown himself moved to the sleepy Virginia community, nestled comfortably at the confluence of the Shenandoah and the Potomac rivers. He arrived by train at Sandy Hook, Maryland, another small rural town located about a mile from Harpers Ferry across the Potomac. Soon after his arrival, he rented a small farm in Maryland that had recently been vacated after the death of the owner, Dr. Robert F. Kennedy. Kennedy had purchased the farm's nearly 200 acres from the Antietam Iron Works just seven years earlier. The farmhouse was a two-story structure that still stands today, "a two hours' walk from the river."[12] Brown passed himself off, along with three of his sons, as Isaac Smith & Sons, cattle investment men from New York. The group claimed to need a farm as a feedlot for cattle to be purchased and fattened up before they were sold. Their true plan was quite different. They would use the Kennedy Farm as the base from which they would stage Brown's misguided raid on the federal arsenal at Harpers Ferry.

Over the following weeks, Brown and his men quietly carried out their plan. They had gathered weapons at a schoolhouse closer to the arsenal than the Kennedy Farm, a cache that included "hundreds of carbines, pistols, spears or pikes, and a quantity of cartridges, powder, percussion caps, and other military supplies, that he [Brown] had gathered for arming the negroes when they rose to insurrection in response to his call and movements."[13]

By Sunday evening, October 16, all was ready. Brown and 16 other white men from Connecticut, New York, Ohio, Iowa, Pennsylvania, Maine, Indiana, and Canada, along with five blacks from Ohio, Pennsylvania, and New York, were fully armed and ready to cross the Potomac River and advance on Harpers Ferry. Two of the black followers were students at Oberlin College in Ohio, an abolitionist institution, the first college in the United States to integrate fully.

Through the night, the 22 men made their move. They loaded a wagon with 1,000 newly manufactured pikes from a factory in Connecticut. Each man carried a rifle and a pair of handguns. They reached the Baltimore & Ohio Railroad bridge by 10 P.M. and advanced on the government armory on the town's east end. A night watchman at the armory heard them come and went out to see what was happening. Brown's men grabbed him and forced him to unlock the armory's gate. One of the raiders climbed a pole and cut the telegraph line that led into the unsuspecting Virginia community. Brown and his small group occupied the armory, even as he informed the guard that he was John Brown from Kansas and he had come to free the slaves of Virginia.

Before long, the raid had its first casualty: Hayward Shepherd, the rail station's baggage handler. The conspirators may not have realized in the darkness that he was one of the town's 150 free blacks. The plot continued to unfold as the conspirators fanned out and overpowered the guards at the arsenal near the train station and at the rifle factory above the town on the banks of the Shenandoah. They then posted guards of their own at those locations and throughout the town itself. Brown took up a position in the thick-walled brick armory building; half of the building provided the living quarters for the armory's night watchman, and the other housed a horse-drawn fire engine. Brown sent men to round up some of the important citizens in the area and to begin to rally local blacks as the raid's first recruits. Among the captives was Colonel L. W. Washington, a nephew of George Washington. Within a few hours, 40 residents of Harpers Ferry and the surrounding countryside were prisoners of the abolitionist conspirators. As for Brown, he halted an eastbound passenger train bound for Baltimore. In the excitement, one of Brown's followers killed the guard at the railroad bridge.

All these incidents did not go on without the realization by townspeople that something curious was under way. Those who first recognized the plot rang church bells to warn their neighbors of a possible slave uprising. By early morning, local citizens had reached the armory in force; they streamed in from the surrounding farms and villages of Virginia and Maryland. As morning raced toward noon on October 17, the Jefferson Guards, a local militia unit, arrived at the armory. The conspirators were holed up inside the engine house, with approximately 10 of their captives with them. From every window and hole in the walls, Brown and his men fired their rifles at the approach of any and all white people in the streets outside. The response of the angry townspeople came as no surprise to Brown. He had told Frederick Douglass, "When I strike the bees will swarm."[14]

Tension was the order of the day as additional militia units reached Harpers Ferry from Baltimore and Frederick, Maryland; and Winchester, Virginia. Late on October 17, a detachment of U.S. Marines arrived on the scene. Throughout the day, stories of the abolitionist assault on the town and the slave revolt that would probably follow had filtered out of Harpers Ferry to the outside world. The stories soon became exaggerations. By the time news reached Washington, D.C., and President James Buchanan, Brown's small force of 21 men had become a racially mixed army of 700 abolitionist firebrands who were arming themselves from the government's armory and preparing for civil war. Buchanan had ordered three artillery companies to Harpers Ferry, along with the aforementioned U.S. Marines. The commander of the federal forces had heard of the Brown raid at his home on the Potomac River at Arlington, Virginia. He had duly received orders "to take command at Harpers Ferry, recapture the government armory and arsenal, and restore order."[15] He was Lieutenant Colonel Robert E. Lee, accompanied by his aide, Lieutenant J. E. B. Stuart, of the First U.S. Cavalry. When Lee reached the town, he found everything in chaos. Many of the men in Harpers Ferry had become drunk throughout the day. Several times, when some of Brown's men tried to surrender with white flags to show their intentions, drunken men had fired on them. One of the first steps Lee took was to close the local taverns and saloons.

MARTYR FOR A CAUSE

By the morning of October 18, John Brown's grand plan to free America's slaves had come to an end. At dawn, Lee ordered a dozen marines to storm the engine house, three of them armed with sledgehammers. When the hammers proved useless (Brown had barricaded the doors with the fire engine), Lee ordered his forward reserves toward the engine house. With a heavy ladder as a battering ram, they shattered one of the doors, and the troops rushed in. The assault only lasted a matter of minutes. Ten of Brown's men were killed immediately or would die later from their wounds. (Lee had ordered his men to use their bayonets to keep civilian casualties to a minimum.) Among those killed were two of Brown's sons. Brown himself was severely wounded when he was slashed by an officer's sword. Brown and six of his men were taken prisoner, and another five escaped, although two were later apprehended. During the assault, the first of Brown's men killed was Dangerfield Newby, a black man.

Brown survived his wounds and stood trial. He was turned over to the Commonwealth of Virginia and faced charges of treason against the commonwealth and of murder. After a weeklong trial, he was found guilty. On December 2, 1859, Brown was hanged. Among those who witnessed his execution was a unit of cadets from the Virginia Military Institute and their commander, Major Thomas J. Jackson, whom history would one day remember as Stonewall Jackson. Jackson later wrote a letter to his wife in which he described Brown as he ascended the steps to the waiting gallows. Brown, Jackson stated, "behaved with unflinching firmness."[16]

Even in death, John Brown would become a symbol for the abolitionist movement. He was a driven idealist whose hatred of slavery, a legally recognized institution in nineteenth-century America, led to extreme violence and to

After a weeklong trial, John Brown was found guilty of treason, murder, and inciting slaves to rebel, and was subsequently hanged on December 2, 1859. Brown is depicted here in Thomas Hovendon's 1882 oil painting, *The Last Moments of John Brown,* which is on display at the Metropolitan Museum of Art in New York City.

his own death as a martyr. Ironically, within just a few short years, slavery would be brought to an end in the United States. It would not happen without further bloodshed. Less than two years after Brown's Harpers Ferry raid, America's North and South would descend into a Civil War that would not end until 620,000 Americans lay dead on battlefields from Virginia to New Mexico. Before the war that ended slavery, however, there was a long, clarion campaign that decried the wrongness of slavery and slaveholding. That campaign was a nationwide movement of men and women whose desire to end slavery would make others call them irresponsible, inflammatory, insistent, and even crazed, like John Brown. They were abolitionists.

Slavery Comes to America

During the centuries before contact between the Old World and the New World, slavery existed in both. American Indians made slaves of those individuals they captured in war, and Europeans did the same. Before Christopher Columbus sailed to America in 1492, Italian merchants and shippers bought and sold people from the Slavic countries of eastern Europe. (The word *slave* is derived from the word *Slav*.) At that same time, however, fifteenth-century Europeans were also trafficking slaves who were Africans or Muslims and sometimes both. This activity was especially encouraged after a fifteenth-century pope excommunicated merchants who sold Slavs who were Christians, as nearly all of them were. This soon caused a shift in the European slave trade, which hinged on the shipment of black Africans to slave markets. According to the historical record, the first black Africans brought to Europe as slaves were delivered to Lisbon, the capital of Portugal, in 1441. Within a few short years, the black slave trade between European traders and African victims was well established.

SLAVES IN THE NEW WORLD

With Columbus's "discovery" of the New World of the Americas and the introduction of sugar to the West Indies, the institution of slavery in the Western Hemisphere soon followed, especially in relation to sugar production. Black slaves were imported to the

Americas as early as 1518, and, by the end of the sixteenth century, 25,000 African slaves "were being worked to death on sugar plantations on the islands of Cuba and Hispaniola, and in South American Brazil."[17] The Spanish and Portuguese imported thousands of black slaves because they provided

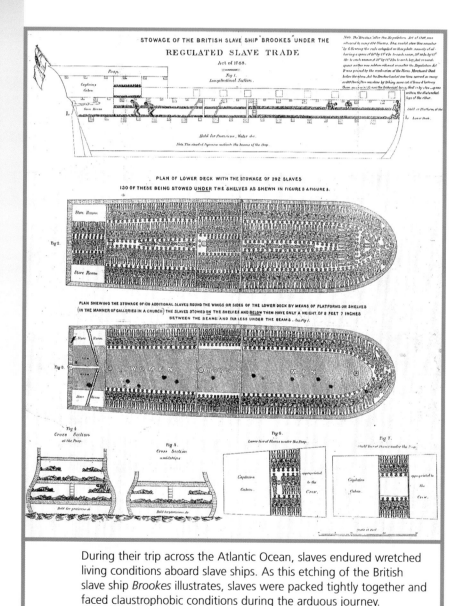

During their trip across the Atlantic Ocean, slaves endured wretched living conditions aboard slave ships. As this etching of the British slave ship *Brookes* illustrates, slaves were packed tightly together and faced claustrophobic conditions during the arduous journey.

an inexpensive workforce. Given the extremely high profits generated by the sale of sugar in Europe, other European powers—including France, Holland, and England—established sugar plantations and refining mills of their own throughout the Caribbean islands.

This trend led to the introduction of millions of black slaves into the New World over the coming centuries. Today, historians estimate that, between 1500 and 1850, 10 million African slaves were imported to the Western Hemisphere. (Possibly another 2 million died during the Middle Passage sea voyage from Africa to the Caribbean Islands.) The peak period of importation took place between 1701 and 1810, years during which three of every four slaves were shipped to the Americas, which included the British colonies along the Atlantic seaboard. The number brought to the British colonies of North America represented approximately only 5 percent of those 10 million who were imported, however. By comparison, about 50 percent were sold for labor on Dutch, British, and French sugar plantations and related work. About one in three were brought to Portuguese Brazil. The Spanish brought over approximately 10 percent of the total number of imported slaves.

SLAVERY IN THE AMERICAN COLONIES

Once the European slave ships completed the Middle Passage from Africa to the Americas, the slaves were brought to one of dozens of possible New World ports. Those slaves eventually bought for service in the British colonies of North America found themselves face-to-face with a world they did not understand, and they had few fellow slaves to cling to for hope. Slavery in the New World was more than a century old before the first African workers were introduced to the British colonies of North America. Jamestown, the first permanent English settlement along the Atlantic Coast, founded in

1607, saw its initial import of Africans in 1619. That year, a Dutch ship, the *Jesus of Lubeck*, docked and traded Africans for some supplies the crew desperately needed. English resident John Rolfe described the introduction of these first black workers to the British colony: "About the last of August came a dutch man of warre that sold us twenty Negars."[18] Such workers were typically used to tend to the tobacco fields throughout the Tidewater region.

These earliest African arrivals, however, were not, by definition, true slaves. Because the institution of slavery did not exist by law in Jamestown, the Africans were considered yet another group of workers. These blacks were not regarded much differently than servants. In fact, they and their children obtained land in time and eventually gained their complete freedom after they paid off their passage to America (never mind that they had not chosen to come to America in the first place). In fact, some of the early black arrivals to Jamestown would later become not only landowners but slaveholders, as well.

From the early organization of the British colonies along the Atlantic Coast of North America, the number of slaves brought to those colonies remained low—that is, until later in the 1700s. In 1700, the number of slaves in British North America constituted about 11 percent of the total (non-Indian) colonial population. By the Revolutionary War (1775–1783), however, the number of slaves had nearly doubled, at 20 percent of the total colonial population.

Slavery Takes Root

As noted, the first black arrivals in the British colonies of North America were typically servants, not viewed much differently from white servants. Long before the end of the seventeenth century, however, the status of African workers

(continues on page 27)

SOUTHERN COLONIES AND SLAVERY

By the mid-1700s, the British colonial south included two larger regions: the Chesapeake, or the Tidewater South, and the Lower South. English colonists had called the Chesapeake (generally Virginia and Maryland) their home longer than those colonists who later migrated into the Lower South, which included the Carolinas and Georgia. Establishment of all the Southern colonies spanned more than a century—from the settlement of Jamestown in Virginia in 1607 to the creation of Georgia as a colonial enterprise in the early 1730s.

During the 1700s, three racial groups dominated the South: whites, most of whom were descendants of earlier English colonists; blacks, the vast majority of whom were slaves held for life; and Native Americans, the first inhabitants of the Atlantic Coast region who still lived on the edge of colonial society. They traded with whites just as their earlier ancestors had during the 1600s.

Although by far, most Southern whites were of English descent, but some had ancestors who had emigrated from other places. Other representative Europeans included Germans, Austrians, Scots, Irish, Welsh, and French. Most of these groups contributed small numbers to the general population. Some, such as the Germans and the Scots, had a greater impact on the part of the South where they concentrated in larger numbers. The Scots, for example, largely settled in North Carolina. Upon taking a closer look at the resulting population of this three-tiered social structure, numbers begin to tell another part of the story. By 1750, black slaves constituted approximately 40 percent of the South's population. This fact reveals the importance of slavery as a labor force throughout the region.

Although early settlement of the South had been along specific parts of the Atlantic seaboard, by the 1700s, people had not only filled in the coastal shorelines but had moved inland and used the multitude of rivers that flowed west to east. This inward migration landed them in the great valleys of the piedmont, just east of the Appalachian Mountains. Most

(continues)

(continued)

of those individuals who inhabited the South, even in the 1700s, still lived in rural places, not in larger cities. They owned farms where they grew the typical crops of the day, which included grains and corn, but more importantly, tobacco, indigo, and rice.

In some parts of the South, people lived on plantations, great farms that became the most significant of all social and economic institutions in the region. By the mid-1700s, a typical Southern plantation included a large house, often established on high ground, with fields that surrounded it in all directions. Outbuildings might include a smokehouse, summer kitchen, barns, stables, corncribs, and drying sheds, where large bundles of tobacco leaves could cure naturally. Slaves worked such large acreages and provided most of the labor for the cultivation of tobacco, which took many hours of field work, most of which was dedicated to clearing the weeds away from the delicate tobacco leaves. Usually, slaves lived in basic wooden cabins with a dirt floor, no windows, and little furniture. Such places were oppressively hot in the summer and cold in the winter. One cabin might be the home of several families who lived together. These cabins were called the "slave quarters."

Although plantations were the most dominant labor and production system in the South, the vast majority of white families did not own a plantation and were not wealthy or powerful. They were poor yeoman farmers who owned their own small acreages and scratched out a living with tobacco, the one primary cash crop of the South. These farmers were small-scale landowners and might have just a few slaves, if any at all.

Typically, these poorer white farmers worked in their own fields alongside their black workers. Because their farm operations were small, such people moved often; they regularly pulled up stakes and reestablished themselves on other lands farther away from the Atlantic Coast. The crop they grew was one reason they moved often. Tobacco is a crop that quickly saps nutrients from the soil. Because these colonial farmers did not use much fertilizer, their farm soil was depleted after four or five tobacco crops.

(continued from page 24)

in the colonies underwent a significant change, with the development of racial attitudes that caused whites to look at blacks in a different way. This attitude was more prominent in the Southern colonies than elsewhere. In 1662, the Virginia House of Burgesses acknowledged the new status by a vote that the children of slave mothers inherited their mother's status, which meant they would be born into slavery. Other colonies did the same. By 1665, in New York, where the English had wrested the colony of New Netherland from the Dutch just the year before, leaders institutionalized slavery for life. In 1671, similar laws that established black slavery were created in Maryland. Over the following decades, slavery was institutionalized in all of the then-existing British colonies on the Atlantic seaboard. By 1705, the colonial legislature enacted a far-reaching Slave Code, "which further defined the duties of slaves, closing nearly every door that might have allowed a black worker to become free."[19] Other colonies soon followed suit and enacted laws similar to those of Virginia. By 1710, black slaves outnumbered white servants in these colonies by five to one.

Slavery Leads to Revolt

As slavery developed and grew into a common institution in the British colonies of North America, more and more innocent victims found themselves living in a world of control, abuse, and degradation. Slaves were often treated as property. They had few rights recognized by law and almost no hope of release from the yoke of white control. This situation sometimes led slaves to rebel against such treatment. Some slaves chose to run away from their masters. Others chose to resist their owners nonviolently, which led them to work slower and become less productive. As one slaveholder wrote, "You would really be surpris'd at their Perseverance. They often die before they can be conquered."[20] Still others elected to rebel outright against the system of slavery.

It was this form of resistance that whites feared the most. A slave rebellion or revolt sometimes meant that whites, as well as blacks, would be killed. Slave revolts were certainly rare compared with the more common rebellion of quiet resistance or even escape. They did, though, occur. During the late British colonial period, two waves of slave revolts occurred in the years 1710 to 1722 and 1730 to 1740. Of the documented slave rebellions during these years, two were most noteworthy. One took place in New York in 1712 and the other in South Carolina in 1739. In the 1712 rebellion, more than two dozen slaves rose up against harsh treatment. They set fire to a building and seized all the weapons they could find. Before it was all over, the slaves had killed nine white men and wounded another six. A local militia unit was called out to put down the slave uprising. Of the 27 involved in the revolt, 21 were executed, and the remaining 6 committed suicide.

The next significant slave uprising in the British colonies of North America took place in the fall of 1739. Known as the Stono Rebellion, the drama unfolded 20 miles outside Charleston, South Carolina, near Stono Bridge. A slave from the African state of Angola led the revolt, which began when a group of slaves raided a "wearehouse, & then plundered it of guns & ammunition."[21] They then cut off the heads of the warehousemen and made a run toward Spanish-held Florida and freedom. Other slaves joined them until they numbered close to 100. As they moved south, they raided plantations and killed as many as 30 whites. A posse of angry whites gave chase to the rebellious slaves; they eventually caught up with some of them and killed 44. Although many of these slaves escaped into the Florida swamps, authorities in

Charleston "arrested 150 slaves and hanged ten daily to quell that spirit."[22]

EARLY ABOLITIONISM

Although such rebellions further strengthened many Southerners' support of slavery, the eighteenth century began to witness some important movements in opposition to the institution. The abolitionist movement traces its roots to the colonial period in America. One of the important factors may have been the sugar market of the period. Although sugar had caused a dramatic buildup of slavery in the New World in earlier centuries, the 1700s experienced wide swings in the price of sugar. This fluctuation had an immediate impact on the importance of slavery as a labor institution. In addition, a philosophical movement called the Enlightenment was developing in western Europe. It began to gain a foothold in the late 1600s and expanded its base of support during the eighteenth century. Those who supported the Enlightenment held a strong "confidence in human reason as a guide to wisdom, a rejection of ignorance and superstition, a firm belief in the basic goodness of humankind, and a certainty that society, through reason, could be perfected."[23] Enlightened Europeans (the movement had supporters in America, as well) came to believe that the laws of nature demanded a natural equality among humans, a principle that defied institutional slavery. The Enlightenment encouraged abolitionism.

There were others, driven by different ideas, such as those of Christianity, who came to believe that slavery was a moral wrong and should be done away with. Among Protestant groups, especially, Christians were led to conclude that slavery was wrong and an injustice. One such group was the Quakers. As early as 1688, a group of Quakers who lived in Germantown, Pennsylvania, preached against slavery. Five years later, Quakers published the first antislavery pamphlet in America. In time, some members of Quaker congregations spoke out against slavery and its evils.

Many Quakers of the late 1600s and early 1700s, however, were not yet ready to admit to the evils of slaveholding. One of the important antislavery Quaker voices was Ralph Sandiford, who published a pamphlet titled *A Brief Examination of the Practice of the Times* in 1729. (It was printed by Benjamin Franklin.) His fellow Quakers rejected his ideas and his writings. Sandiford died four years later. In 1737, another Quaker writer, Benjamin Lay, published *All Slave-Keepers That Keep the Innocent in Bondage, Apostates*. These early antislavery works, though, were not even accepted by the majority of Quakers, "many of whom trafficked in and owned slaves."[24] As for Lay, many of his fellow Quakers would not allow him to attend their meetings. However, by the mid-1700s, because of these earlier writings and others that came later, Quakers turned against slavery. As a group, they no longer bought slaves. By the 1760s, they began to free their slaves, as well. Their call, however, was not for abolition, but for gradual emancipation. In 1775, the year the Revolutionary War began, an organization called the Society for the Relief of Free Negroes Unlawfully Held in Bondage was formed. It was founded in Philadelphia, and the majority of its members (16 of 24) were Quakers.

SLAVERY AND THE REVOLUTIONARY WAR

By the mid-eighteenth century, slavery was still an important part of the economies of all the British colonies along the Atlantic Coast, especially those of the South, where 90 percent of the slaves lived. It was well defined by law because it provided a basic labor force. More slaves

Unlike those who toiled on the sugar plantations of the Caribbean, the slaves who worked the fields of the Southern colonies were less expendable, because crops such as tobacco were not as profitable as sugar. Here, slaves are depicted working on an American tobacco plantation in the early 1700s.

were delivered during each decade of the 1700s (Eighty-thousand slaves were imported between 1700 and 1770 to Virginia and Maryland alone.) The slave population expanded accordingly, but even greater numbers of slaves were produced by natural increase—slave women had babies. In fact, the British colonies along the Atlantic Coast were the "first in the Americas to develop slave populations that grew without constant additional imports of fresh slaves to the colonies."[25] It occurred in those colonies only because the slaves delivered there were never treated as expendable, as they were in the Caribbean or South America. The profits from North American agriculture, even tobacco, were not so high that slaves paid for themselves through their labor in just a few years. These circumstances allowed slaves along the Atlantic Coast of the British colonies to replace themselves and even expand their numbers.

By the 1760s and 1770s, these same colonies were poised for extraordinary change. During those decades, the British Crown, embodied in King George III and Parliament, pushed new taxes and customs duties on its American colonies, which caused colonial subjects to feel oppressed. Much unrest from Massachusetts to Georgia resulted; as protests became common, patriot groups, such as the Sons of Liberty, were formed, and civil disobedience against the British increased. By the spring of 1775, British Redcoats and Massachusetts colonial militiamen exchanged musket fire on the village green in the sleepy Massachusetts town of Lexington, and the Revolutionary War began. With the advent of the war, one that would be fought for American independence from Great Britain, the colonists began to view slavery through a new filter.

3

Rebirth of Slavery

As the revolution expanded, the words freedom and liberty could be heard everywhere. With this newfound drive to separate from the British and make their own way freely in the world, some colonial patriots began to view slavery differently. To some, it did not seem right to campaign and even fight for American freedom from the British while the ownership of black human beings was supported. One early patriot leader and pamphlet writer, James Otis, noted: "The Colonists are by law of Nature free born as indeed all men are, white or black. . . . Does it follow that 'tis right to enslave a man because he is black?"[26] Another patriot pamphleteer, Thomas Paine, who wrote some of the most important essays of the revolution, which included *Common Sense*, noted that some patriots "complain so loudly of attempts to enslave them," while at the same time they "hold so many hundred thousands in slavery; and annually enslave many thousands more."[27] Benjamin Rush, a signer of the Declaration of Independence, which declared "all men are created equal," argued with his fellow patriots that "the plant of liberty is of so tender a nature, that it cannot thrive long in the neighborhood of slavery."[28]

In the Revolutionary War, blacks served in uniform and were allowed to fight for the cause of freedom. Others fought to bring

Approximately 5,000 black soldiers participated in the Revolutionary War, fighting for both the colonies and Great Britain. One of the most famous black soldiers was Peter Salem, a former slave who participated in the Battle of Concord and the Battle of Bunker Hill. He is depicted here by American artist J. E. Taylor in his 1899 painting, *Peter Salem Shooting Major Pitcairn at Bunker Hill.*

an end to slavery in the North as colonies became states in the new United States of America. African Americans in Massachusetts, New Hampshire, and Connecticut petitioned their colonial and later state legislatures to consider gradual emancipation. As for those who fought in the Continental Army, black patriots served in integrated field units, with only a couple of exceptions, such as a black Rhode Island regiment and some Massachusetts companies. Estimates place the number of black soldiers who fought on the American side during the Revolutionary War at approximately 5,000. Many of those blacks who were slaves fought to gain their freedom.

Once they did so, they sometimes changed their names, such as Jeffery, Pomp, and Sharp Liberty, and Ned, Cuff, and Peter Freedom.

CHANGE OF HEART OVER SLAVERY

During the years immediately after the Revolutionary War, abolitionism found support in the former British colonies, now new states, of North America. Across the Northern states, the drive was to bring slavery to an end. In 1784, the Pennsylvania Society for the Abolition of Slavery was established, thanks in part to Benjamin Franklin. Earlier in his life, Franklin had actually owned one or two slaves, but he had come to believe, because of the ideals of the Enlightenment, that slavery was wrong. Fellow organizers included such Founding Fathers as Alexander Hamilton (the first secretary of the treasury) and John Jay (the first chief justice of the U.S. Supreme Court). The following year, Jay served as president of another organization, the New York Manumission Society. Within a decade, these two Northern antislavery institutions joined forces to form the American Convention for Promoting the Abolition of Slavery and Improving the Condition of the African Race. Such groups did not actively campaign against slavery to any real degree. Instead, they believed that slavery was destined to die out within a short time. The Revolutionary War had encouraged such ideals as liberty and independence, and slaveholding seemed at odds with those ideals. "Nothing is more certainly written in the book of fate than that these people are to be free,"[29] wrote Founding Father Thomas Jefferson. He and others, Northerners and Southerners alike, believed that slavery's days were numbered and that the institution was headed toward extinction even in the slave states of the South, where tobacco had worn out the fields.

Perhaps even more significant as a sign of slavery's decline were the steps taken by Northern states to do away with the institution on their soil. The end of slavery began even before American victory in the Revolutionary War was ensured. Vermont took the lead by abolishing slavery in 1777. Another New England state, Massachusetts (of which Maine was still a part at that point), included abolition in its state constitution three years later. In 1783, New Hampshire declared itself a nonslaveholding state. In other Northern states, slavery was placed on the clock, to be phased out with gradual abolition. These states included Pennsylvania in 1780; Connecticut and Rhode Island, where large-farm slavery existed, in 1784; New York in 1799; and New Jersey in 1804.

Other telltale signs during the latter decades of the eighteenth century indicated that slavery might soon come to an end. The Constitution permitted Congress to ban the international slave trade, which was then officially abolished after 1808. The new national government that emerged following the Revolutionary War, the Congress of the Confederation, adopted the Northwest Ordinance of 1787. This piece of legislation demanded that the spread of slavery be halted in the great expanses of the Northwest Territory (which included the modern-day states of Ohio, Indiana, Illinois, Michigan, and Wisconsin). Despite the block on slavery established by the Northwest Ordinance of 1787, another act of Congress—the Southwest Ordinance of 1790—allowed for the expansion of slavery in the South, particularly in the territories south of the Ohio River, such as the future states of Tennessee, Kentucky, Mississippi, and Alabama. These places were granted the right to hold slaves because it was assumed that slavery would take root where the warmer climate and good, rich soil helped support slave-based farming.

Few believed slavery would move quickly into these future American territories because no one foresaw the possibilities of cotton production across the South, which would become widespread during the beginning of the nineteenth century. The invention of the cotton gin by a Northerner named Eli Whitney made certain of that.

MOMENTOUS INVENTION

Slavery was rescued in the late eighteenth century, perhaps ironically, by a tinkering mechanic, a graduate of Yale University, who visited a plantation near Savannah, Georgia, in 1792. Eli Whitney had gone to the South to take a job as a tutor but turned it down after a misunderstanding about his salary. In the meantime, he had struck up a friendship with the plantation's owner, Catherine Greene, the widow of Revolutionary War general Nathaniel Greene. While there, he was asked by the widow Greene if he could try to build a device to remove the sticky green seeds from upland cotton. The plant grew well in the region but was not practical as a crop because of the labor needed to clean cotton bolls of their seeds, even though "Whitney had never seen a cotton boll."[30] He gave it a try. "In about 10 days," Whitney would later write, "I made a little model, for which I was offered, if I would give up all right and title to it, a Hundred Guineas. . . . I concluded to . . . turn my attention to perfecting the Machine."[31] The Northern mechanic had invented a device he would call the "cotton engine," or "gin" for short.

Few inventions in American history have had a greater impact. It was a simple contraption, fashioned from wood and a wire screen. It was little more than a "device that used toothed cylinders to snag the lint through a wire screen,

With the invention of the cotton gin in the early 1800s, Eli Whitney reinvigorated the cotton industry by making it easier for the seeds to be removed from the fiber. The first cotton gin is depicted in this engraving, which appeared in the December 18, 1869, edition of *Harper's Weekly.*

leaving the seeds behind."[32] Overnight, the production of American cotton would increase substantially. Whereas it took a slave 10 hours to clean the seeds from 1 pound of cotton lint, Whitney's "perfected" model could produce between 300 and 1,000 pounds of cleaned cotton fiber in a day. By the mid-1790s, the South, with the use of slave labor, was exporting more than 1.6 million pounds of cotton, most of it to England's textile mills. The explosion in cotton production would continue through the decades to follow. By 1850, Southern cotton production reached a million tons annually. Slavery had become essential to the Southern economy. One nineteenth-century senator from

South Carolina, James Henry Hammond, would announce to the world: "Cotton is King and the African must be a slave, or there's an end of all things, and soon."[33]

POSTWAR OPPOSITION TO SLAVERY

Undoubtedly, the abolitionist cause remained limited and tenuous in the generation after the end of the Revolutionary War. Various antislavery societies had been established by the early 1790s, most of them ironically in the South. They met occasionally and irregularly and mostly petitioned state governments to establish schools to educate blacks. They also wrote and otherwise campaigned against the African slave trade. Southern abolitionists "undoubtedly aided fugitives to escape."[34] This antislavery sentiment continued into the early nineteenth century.

During these years, the goal was generally not the abolition of slavery but the gradual freedom of the existing slave population. There was no loud demand to much of it and no "particular urgency to it."[35] The assumption that those slaves who were freed would not stay in the United States usually ran alongside any campaign to reduce the scope of slavery and free slave groups. Even the majority of those who thought the goal of freedom for slaves was a decent and morally positive idea did not believe those free blacks should remain on American soil. Groups were formed whose goal was to return free blacks to Africa. One of the most important of such groups was the American Colonization Society, which was established in 1816 (see sidebar on pages 40–43). Its stated goal was to "send ex-bondsmen out of the country, preferably to its African outpost, Liberia."[36] Politicians, important individuals, and even slaveholders

(continues on page 43)

COLONIZATION IN LIBERIA

Perhaps the most important antislavery organization in the United States during the 1810s and 1820s was the American Society for Colonizing the Free People of Color of the United States. The organization was not simply interested in the antislavery position. It was concerned about what to do with slaves once they were free. The organization's solution was to ship them back to Africa.

The organization was founded late in 1816 in Washington, D.C., by whites, some of them quite prominent, such as Congressman Henry Clay and Supreme Court Justice Bushrod Washington, the nephew of George Washington. Other important Americans would support the group and its efforts, such as future presidents Andrew Jackson and John Tyler, and Francis Scott Key, the Baltimore lawyer who wrote "The Star-Spangled Banner." Such important white men as U.S. Representative Daniel Webster of New Hampshire (he would later be a senator from Massachusetts); Secretary of State and later President James Monroe; and South Carolina Representative and later Senator John C. Calhoun were members. Many of the group's earlier members came from the Upper South. By the 1820s, there were branch chapters in every Northern state. During the 1820s, even William Lloyd Garrison was a supporter, although he would change his position by the following decade. He and John C. Calhoun would become spokesmen for two completely different groups. Garrison would lead the abolitionist cause against slavery, whereas Calhoun, as a vocal Southern politician, would become one of slavery's most vocal supporters. Calhoun believed passionately that blacks were inferior to whites and that their inherent inferiority left them ill equipped to fend for themselves. Whites did blacks a favor, Calhoun believed, in their maintenance of them as slaves. His support of colonization only addressed his belief that freed blacks had no place in a white America. Instead, they should return to Africa.

Popularly known as the American Colonization Society (ACS), the group had a dual purpose. One purpose was to help bring about the abolition of slavery, not at once, but gradually, in the United States. The organization talked of how to compensate slaveholders for the loss of their slaves in a way that would be fair. Second, once slaves were freed

The American Colonization Society (depicted here) was established in 1816 by Reverend Robert Finley to serve as a vehicle to establish a colony for free blacks in the African country of Liberia. However, most free blacks chose to stay in the United States, and by the eve of the Civil War, only 10,000 had returned to Africa.

a program would be in place to "send emancipated slaves and free black people to Liberia."* This second purpose was based on the understanding that slave masters would never free their slaves in large numbers if it would result in a large free population of blacks in America. Many whites did not believe the races—black and white—could live side by side without the institution of slavery.

Some free blacks in the North were not as accepting of the ACS as whites often were. Northern blacks were keenly aware that their rights as American blacks were rarely guaranteed, and they saw the ACS as a means to circumvent their rights by their removal from America altogether. In 1817, 3,000 black opponents met in Philadelphia at Bethel Church to protest and denounce the society. They asserted their rights as black citizens, rights they believed they had fought for and gained through their military

(continues)

(continued)

service in the Revolutionary War and the War of 1812. They had defended the cause of American freedom themselves and were not about to lose their freedom and be shipped to a land of which they had no living memory.

Despite such protests against the idea and goal of colonization back to Africa, some prominent black abolitionists supported the organization. Indeed, some blacks had given support to the concept of the return of American blacks to Africa before the founding of the ACS. In 1811, a black Quaker of mixed African and American Indian descent, Paul Cuffe, presented the subject before a session of Congress. Men such as Cuffe agreed with the sentiment that "white prejudice would never allow black people to enjoy full citizenship, equal protection under the law, and economic success in the United States."** Other black leaders agreed. "[Blacks] would never become a people," argued James Forten, who chaired the Bethel Church meeting, "until they come out from amongst the white people."***

Cuffe pursued on his own the goal of colonization even before the ACS was formed. In 1815, Cuffe, who had his own ship, recruited 34 blacks in America to sail to the British free black colony of Sierra Leone, in West Africa, northwest of Liberia. (Cuffe might have settled there himself, except that his American Indian wife would not leave her homeland.) By the next year, the ACS was founded, and Cuffe's example served as an incentive.

By 1820, backed by financial support from the U.S. government, a prominent black bishop of the African Methodist Episcopal Church (AME), Daniel Coker, delivered 86 African Americans to the West African coast on a ship named the *Mayflower of Liberia*. The following year, another group of black colonists from the First Baptist Church CF Richmond, Virginia, a racially mixed congregation, left for Liberia under the leadership of Lott Cary, a former slave who had purchased his own freedom. Although born in America, Carry was convinced that blacks in the United States would never succeed because of white hatred. Migrating to Africa made perfect sense. "I am an African," he claimed, and he went to Africa in the hope that he would connect with the continent of his ancestors and find opportunities denied

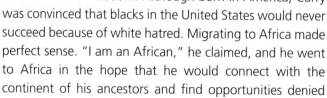

him in America. Such migrations from the United States to Africa were, however, rare. Over the next two decades, approximately 2,500 blacks migrated willingly from the United States to Liberia. (At the time, the number of Liberian natives stood possibly at fewer than 30,000.)

The number of blacks who left the United States for a new life in Liberia was never significant. By 1860, the year before the start of the American Civil War, only 10,000 American blacks had left American soil for Africa. This number represents "just .3 percent of the increase of the black population in the United States since 1816,"[†] the year the ACS was founded. Other colonizing efforts were made to other international destinations. During the later 1820s, the president of the Caribbean island nation of Haiti, Jean-Pierre Boyer, invited black Americans to migrate to his country, which was largely inhabited by blacks whose ancestors had reached the island during the days of Spanish-controlled slavery. Thousands accepted the invitation.

---

[*] Darlene Clark Hine, *The African-American Odyssey* (Upper Saddle River, N.J.: Prentice Hall 2005), 176.
[**] Ibid., 177.
[***] James Oliver Horton and Lois E. Horton, *Slavery and the Making of America* (New York: Oxford University Press, 2005), 91.
[†] Hine, 177.

(continued from page 39)
themselves numbered among the members of this group. The society included those who supported slavery but wanted to remove the free black population from the United States, as well as those who opposed slavery but did not believe that blacks and whites could live side by side. Unfortunately, the primary goal of the society was "to get rid of black people."[37] During 10 or 15 years, the society managed to send a few blacks back to Africa.

New Age of Abolitionism

Prior to 1819, slavery, with its long history as an American institution, was hardly an important political issue in the United States. It would fail to divide the country then as it would in later decades. Slavery could scarcely be called a cause for division between the North and South. However, developing events would thrust slavery to the forefront of the American political stage during the coming years.

NEW LANDS OPEN TO SLAVERY

In the years leading up to 1819, slavery was becoming more prominent. The anticipation of slavery's decline along with a waning tobacco economy were no longer a reality. A new burgeoning cotton market was driving the South's economy. Southern planters raced one another to plant new fields of the profitable white fiber. Because cotton production, like tobacco crops, wore out the soil after just a few years, a scramble for new lands to the west unfolded. Between 1787, the year the U.S. Constitution was written, and 1819, five new slave states had been added to the Union: Kentucky, Tennessee, Louisiana, Mississippi, and Alabama. Slave numbers grew dramatically during the early decades of the 1800s. Tennessee's slave population in 1790 was approximately 3,000, but, by 1830, that number had risen to more than 140,000. The number of slaves in Mississippi stood at 3,000 in 1800 but, by 1830, had increased to more than 65,000. In 1819, a new territory, Florida, was annexed to the United States through a treaty made with Spain. Before long, slavery would find its way farther west. Southerners, in their search for even more land for cotton cultivation, looked west of the Mississippi, to the Missouri Territory.

Since the purchase of the Louisiana Territory in 1803 from the French (Missouri was part of the purchased territory, as was the slave state of Louisiana), the majority of Northerners had believed that slavery would not spread in that direction. Missouri was too far north, its climate hardly that of a true Southern state. By 1819, however, the leadership of Missouri had fallen into the hands of those who owned slaves and wanted to bring slavery to the region. They pushed for Missouri to be granted admission into the Union as a slave state.

THE MISSOURI COMPROMISE

Northerners refused to stand by and watch slavery take root in yet another new territory. In February 1819, a Republican congressman from New York, James Tallmadge, proposed an amendment to be accepted as a restriction on Missouri's statehood application. The amendment banned future slave imports into Missouri and a plan of eventual emancipation for the slaves already held in the territory. The amendment was rejected by most Southerners, as well as Missourians. The federal government should have no voice in whether Missouri was admitted as a free or slave state, they said. Such interference was unconstitutional, because states, proslavery advocates argued, had the absolute right to draft their proposed constitutions any way they saw fit.

The drive to admit Missouri as a slave state stalled. The vote followed sectional lines; Northerners passed the amendment in the House of Representatives, and Southerners blocked it in the Senate. (At that time, representation in the Senate was evenly split between the number of slave and free states. Southerners became agitated at the attempt to block Missouri's admission as a slave state because they knew its status as such would tip the balance in the Senate their way.) Months of debate ensued. Emotions became so volatile that some Southerners even spoke of the separation of the South from the Union through secession.

The clash over Missouri was not resolved during the 1819 session and was held over into the following congressional session. Then, in the spring of 1820, Speaker of the House Henry Clay proposed a compromise. The compromise took away all restrictions regarding slavery in Missouri and allowed it to enter as a slave state, balanced by the admission of another free state, Maine, which was then part of the New England state of Massachusetts. This arrangement would maintain a balance in the Senate between the number of slave and free states. In exchange for a Northern concession that allowed Missouri slave state status, slavery was banned from the remainder of the Louisiana Purchase territory north of the 36°30' parallel, which was the southern boundary of Missouri. This ban would close off slavery to the remainder of the territory, with the exception of Arkansas Territory (which then included Indian Territory—present-day Oklahoma). Clay's compromise had something for everyone, and the impasse blocking Missouri statehood was overcome.

The agreement, however, almost collapsed when, in November, Missourians submitted a constitution that banned all free blacks from entering Missouri. This ban raised an immediate protest from Northerners who argued that the mandate denied free blacks their rights as citizens under the

In 1820, Speaker of the House Henry Clay (depicted here) proposed the Missouri Compromise, which allowed Maine to enter the Union as a free state and Missouri as a slave state. It also guaranteed that slavery would not be permitted in any future state north of Missouri's southern border.

U.S. Constitution. Southerners were quick to note that, even in Northern states, blacks were not permitted to vote and serve in state militias. Eventually, the North accepted the proposed Missouri constitution. After all, most Americans, Southerners and Northerners alike, did not believe blacks were equal to whites, and violation of the rights of blacks did not offend that many whites. Clay's Missouri Compromise was saved "by sacrificing the claims of free black citizens for equal treatment."[38]

Even though the Missouri Compromise resulted in the admission of Missouri as a slave state, white Southerners were not completely happy with the agreement. They understood that it was only a matter of time before they would be outnumbered by free states and become a political minority. They were already a numerical minority, with the Northern states growing in population (due largely to European immigration) faster than the South. In the House, the percentage of representatives from the South to that of the North was already only two to five. During the months of debate over Missouri's application for statehood, Southern congressmen witnessed "the crystallization in Congress of a northern majority array against the expansion of slavery."[39] A struggle was developing between two geographical sections of the United States, the North and the South, over the expansion of slavery into another section of the Union—the West. Where the struggle would take the United States in the future, no one could predict.

Former president Thomas Jefferson was among those Southerners who did not see the Missouri Compromise in a positive light. He believed the compromise represented "a dangerous principle" and wrote in a private letter that the territorial agreement rang, to him, "like a fire bell in the night."[40] Jefferson predicted future tensions between North and South over the issue and the expansion of slavery that he believed would lead to extreme conflict in the United States. He was uncertain what steps should be taken to avoid the inevitable clash. Simply to end slavery was unacceptable to him. He was convinced that slaveholding was wrong, but he could not imagine that former slaves would be accepted into white society. If slavery was preserved, however, it would certainly breed conflict. To find a solution would not be easy, he thought. It was, he wrote, as though we were to hold a "wolf by the ears, and we can neither hold him, nor safely let him go."[41]

EARLY VOICES IN SUPPORT OF ABOLITION

Although many whites, both in the North and South, did little to push the cause of abolition during the early decades of the 1800s, some led the way toward the kind of antislavery movement that would become established by the early 1830s. Several people were singularly important, many of whom were Southerners. David Rice, a Southern minister, spoke out against slavery and called it an "injustice and robbery."[42] Another minister, a Virginia Baptist named David Barrow, was removed from his church's association because he preached in favor of freedom for slaves. Yet another minister from Virginia, John D. Paxton, a Presbyterian, spoke of the "moral evil of slavery and the duty of Christians to aid them and free them."[43] Politicians sided with the cause to free slaves, as well. One such person was Henry Clay, a longtime U.S. congressman who later would become a senator. (He was, however, not an abolitionist, and instead supported gradual emancipation.) Another political figure was James G. Birney, a fellow Kentuckian. He was an attorney who, in state politics, worked to pass legislation to improve the conditions of slaves, even though he was a slaveholder himself. By the 1840s, he would take up the cause of abolition and run for president as the candidate of the new Liberty Party, which sought to end slavery. Other politicians—Daniel Raymond of Maryland, Daniel Bryan and John Randolph of Virginia, and Thomas Hart Benton of Missouri—also challenged slavery.

In Ohio, a strong antislavery group of supporters organized under the leadership of John Rankin, a clergyman who was sometimes referred to as "the father of abolitionism."[44]

He was a native of Tennessee who moved to Kentucky, where he served as a minister in the town of Carlisle from 1817 to 1821. From there, he moved to Ripley, Ohio, where he stayed and preached for the next 44 years. Abolitionism was part of his ministry from his earliest days. In 1814, while in Tennessee, he had been a member of a group that advocated immediate emancipation. In Kentucky, he had helped found societies associated with the Kentucky Abolition Society. Within five years, he was publishing antislavery works. From 1823 through 1824, Rankin published several letters about slavery in a newspaper called the *Castigator*. They were later issued in a popular book that sold many copies in both Kentucky and Tennessee. The letters would be published again in a later, important abolitionist newspaper, *The Liberator*.

The message of Rankin's letters is clear. In them he expresses his absolute hatred for slavery. It was an institution that degraded its victims and that was based completely on racism. As a minister, he felt compelled to explain that blacks were not created to be slaves, as many whites during the nineteenth century believed. He did not support the assumption by some whites that the best option for blacks in the United States was to return to Africa. Instead, he argued that it was not just or right for anyone to own slaves.

Reverend Rankin and Mrs. Stowe

Reverend Rankin became one of the most active agents for the Underground Railroad, a system of safe houses and destinations that were linked together and provided a series of routes that runaway slaves could use to make their way from the South into a more hospitable North. Over the years, Rankin helped thousands of slaves escape bondage. His house was on one of the most important routes for

John Rankin, a Presbyterian minister and abolitionist, was the most prominent conductor on Ohio's Underground Railroad. Rankin's home (pictured here) stands atop a hill above the Ohio River, directly across from Kentucky. From this hilltop location, he could signal to slaves that it was safe to cross the river to Ohio.

slaves who fled their masters, bound for freedom. His home was in Ripley, Ohio, just 50 miles farther up the Ohio River from Cincinnati. In 1828, he purchased 65 acres that fronted the Ohio River, just outside Ripley, and here he established "the first station on the Underground Railroad."[45]

From his house, Reverend Rankin literally shone the light of freedom. In a window on the second story of his home, he placed a lantern that served as a signal to runaways that they had reached a safe house. In a short time, escaped slaves called Rankin's house "Liberty Hill." Hundreds of slaves made their way to the Rankin home, and, in time, approximately 2,000 slaves reached freedom in the North by passing through Rankin's house or through neighboring Ripley.

Rankin's impact extended even beyond his work as a conductor for the Underground Railroad. He figures prominently in the writing of one of the most important books of antislavery sentiment in the United States prior to the Civil War. This book, although not written by Rankin, would help spread his cause even further than his other abolitionist activities. In the autumn of 1834, the Cincinnati Presbyterian Synod conducted its annual meeting in the church, where Reverend Rankin served as minister. Among the attending delegates was Lyman Beecher. Beecher was originally from Boston but had recently moved to Ohio. Reverend Beecher was one of the best-known abolitionists of his day.

Reverend Beecher was accompanied on his trip to Ripley by his daughter Harriet Beecher. She and her father were special guests of Reverend Rankin, and they stayed at his home. She would later write of the days she spent at the minister's home along the Ohio, "gazing over the broad river to the golden Kentucky hills."[46] Among the other guests who stayed at Rankin's home was another minister, a young college professor named Calvin Stowe.

During one of the evenings spent in the Rankin parlor, the abolitionist minister told a story that young Harriet Beecher would never forget. He related a tale of a young slave woman who had made the decision to escape from the Kentucky plantation where she was held and make her way north toward the Ohio River and freedom on the northern side of the river. She chose to leave in late winter. The Ohio River, having been frozen earlier, was already beginning to thaw, which created sheets of disconnected ice. Intent on escape, despite the hazards, the slave woman left her plantation, her baby cradled in her arms, and headed for the place along the Ohio she had been told represented a safe haven—Reverend Rankin's house.

She reached the river at night, and her escape became treacherous. She "ran onto the black river. . . . Slipping and falling on the melting ice, she floundered on, guided by the lone light on the hilltop."[47] She valiantly pushed on under these harsh, dangerous circumstances until she reached the warmth and comfort of the Rankin home. Upon reaching the house, she was welcomed and received a change of clothing while her clothes dried near Rankin's kitchen stove. She was then escorted to the next station on the Underground Railroad. That she had crossed the river successfully was a miracle because the next morning dawned with the river ice completely broken apart, which made another such journey across the river impossible. Those slave catchers who failed to seize her the night before were certain that she had surely drowned in the frigid waters of the Ohio.

Young Harriet Beecher would remember the amazing story that Reverend Rankin spun in his parlor that fall day, the story of a young slave woman who jumped from one mass of ice to another. Years later, after she had married Professor Stowe, she took up the cause of abolitionism as part of her life's work. To that end, she penned, in 1851, one of the most popular of all nineteenth-century American novels. It was a story of slavery she named after the book's title character, a kind and elderly slave named Uncle Tom.

Uncle Tom's Cabin became a runaway best seller: more than 100,000 copies were sold in just three months in 1852. Unlike every other American novel of that era, Harriet Beecher Stowe's book portrayed slaves sympathetically, including Uncle Tom, who is mistreated by his master to the point of death. The book also had a black slave character named Eliza Harris, who would make a decision to escape slavery and make a "midnight crossing of the ice-strewn river."[48] Through the pen of Harriet Beecher Stowe, Reverend Rankin's story would gain a boundless audience

135,000 SETS, 270,000 VOLUMES SOLD.

UNCLE TOM'S CABIN

FOR SALE HERE.

AN EDITION FOR THE MILLION, COMPLETE IN 1 Vol., PRICE 37 1-2 CENTS.
"   "   IN GERMAN, IN 1 Vol., PRICE 50 CENTS.
"   "   IN 2 Vols,. CLOTH, 6 PLATES, PRICE $1.50.
SUPERB ILLUSTRATED EDITION, IN 1 Vol., WITH 153 ENGRAVINGS,
PRICES FROM $2.50 TO $5.00.

The Greatest Book of the Age.

Published in book form in 1852, Harriet Beecher Stowe's *Uncle Tom's Cabin, or Life Among the Lowly,* became an immediate best seller. In contrast to many of her contemporaries, Stowe was sympathetic to the plight of slaves, and the book served to garner support for abolition.

and advance the cause of abolitionism into the hearts of more and more Americans.

Quaker Voice of Abolition

Among the Southerners who battled against the evils of slavery in the early years of the nineteenth century, perhaps none was as important and influential as a Quaker named Benjamin Lundy. Born in New Jersey, he later lived in Wheeling, Virginia (today West Virginia), where he became convinced, at the age of 19, of the importance of abolitionism. For the remainder of his life, he was a tireless campaigner and leader in the cause of abolitionism. He is recognized as one of "the first to establish anti-slavery periodicals, to deliver anti-slavery lectures, and probably to encourage societies for free labor."[49] In 1815, he founded the Union Humane Society in Ohio, where he was a new resident. By 1824, on the lecture circuit, he delivered a series of speeches on slavery and its wrongs. Those speeches led to the establishment of a dozen or more antislavery societies in North Carolina alone. During his lifetime, Lundy "lectured in almost every state in the Union."[50] He established antislavery chapters throughout the country, often in regions where slavery was practiced. Some of those who joined his groups were themselves slaveholders.

In 1828, Lundy made an important acquaintance. While on a Northern lecture tour, which included stops in Philadelphia, New York, Boston, and Providence, Rhode Island, Lundy met another slavery opponent named William Lloyd Garrison, a 23-year-old abolitionist from Massachusetts. Over time, the two would form an important bond. In a published work, Garrison would later describe his first meeting with Lundy. He was disappointed to see that the outspoken abolitionist leader was such a small man. Garrison described how Lundy was so small that "instead of being able to withstand the tide of public opinion it would at first seem doubtful whether he could sustain a temporary conflict with the winds of heaven."[51] Garrison's admiration for Lundy and his work, however, is clear. He gave credit to Lundy, who "explored nineteen of the twenty-four states" and "multiplied anti-slavery societies in every quarter."[52]

Most of Lundy's efforts were centered on his antislavery writings. He wrote his first editorial against slavery in 1817. By the summer of 1821, he began to publish his own abolitionist newspaper, the *Genius of Universal Emancipation*, which he would continue to publish for the next 15 years. Lundy began publication of his paper at Mount Pleasant, Ohio, only to move his base to Greenville, Tennessee, after a few months. By 1824, he shifted publication to Baltimore, Maryland, where it would remain for the next six years. Then, in the fall of 1830, Lundy moved his newspaper offices to Washington, D.C. Four years later, Philadelphia became home to the *Genius* for the next two years. Originally, the *Genius* was published once a month, then twice a month, then monthly again. On July 4, 1825, Lundy changed publication to weekly and enlarged the paper to a size closer to that of newspapers today.

In the pages of the *Genius*, Lundy laid out his agenda for the opposition to slavery. Through a series of seven articles, his program of "immediate gradualism" took form. It included the following provisions: (1) The national government should abolish slavery everywhere Congress had exclusive control, such as all territories and Washington, D.C., and allow no new slave states to enter the Union; (2) the transport of slaves from one state to another should be banned; (3) free states must allow blacks to enter with rights equal to those of whites; (4) aid should be provided to all blacks who want to leave the United States to live elsewhere; (5) all slave states should establish programs of gradual emancipation; (6) slave representation in Congress, which counts slaves only as three-fifths of a person, should be abolished; and (7) a regular convention should be established as a watchdog for all these changes. Although Lundy would, in later years, change some of these ideas (he came to believe in compulsory colonization), he fought for years to achieve these goals.

Perhaps more than any other antislavery newspaper of the 1820s, the *Genius of Universal Emancipation* had a dramatic impact on Americans' view of slavery. For 23 years, Lundy campaigned, until his death in 1839. The voice to follow his was that of William Lloyd Garrison.

5

The Making of an Abolitionist

During Benjamin Lundy's 1828 visit to Boston, he and Garrison met, and it was an encounter that would have a dramatic impact on Garrison's future role as an opponent of slavery. Garrison had already become convinced that gradual abolition was "neither practical nor moral."[53] It was not practical because the very idea of gradualism only delayed the time when general emancipation would take place. It was immoral because "it encouraged slaveholders to go on sinfully and criminally oppressing African Americans."[54] Lundy convinced Garrison to leave his native Massachusetts and move to Baltimore and become the associate editor of the *Genius*. Garrison accepted. By September 1829, Garrison was in Baltimore and was working for the *Genius*. He would redirect the paper and guide its agenda more toward a complete abolitionist track. These Garrison-led issues of the *Genius* covered everything related to slavery, from the harshness of slave conditions to acts of violence made against antislavery newspaper publishers like him. His partnership with Lundy did not last long, however, for Garrison and Lundy went their separate ways in the spring of 1830.

Without question, Garrison had been influenced during the late 1820s by Benjamin Lundy. There would be other influences as well. Two such influences were black abolitionists—fellow newspaper publisher David Walker and a slave named Nat Turner.

INSPIRING WRITER

David Walker was from Wilmington, North Carolina, "a tall, slender, dark-skinned dealer in clothes, new and secondhand,"[55] who moved to Boston to take up his work against slavery. His fiery writings were meant to convince blacks to rebel from slavery during the 1820s. He would inspire later abolitionists who rose to prominence during the 1830s, 1840s, and 1850s, including Garrison. In 1829, Walker published the *Appeal to the Colored Citizens of the World*. In its pages, the controversial black publisher included lurid stories of how slaves were mistreated by their masters. He encouraged black men to stand up against violence perpetrated against their families. In one editorial, Walker wrote, "Had you not rather be killed than be a slave to a tyrant, who takes the life of your mother, wife and dear little children?"[56] Above all, the fiery Walker relentlessly attacked slavery, its wrongs, and the racism of whites. Violence was an option to Walker: "I do declare that one good black can put to death six white men."[57] Such words were especially disturbing to whites in the South, where the *Appeal* circulated among blacks in Southern ports. Even when Walker died in 1830, the influence of the *Appeal* continued for years.

In his writings, Walker had an impact on Garrison specifically, but he had an overall effect on the antislavery movement in general. Early on, Garrison and others had sought to bring about abolition by quiet, peaceful means. Walker advocated anything but that. In his later writings, Garrison became much more militant and supportive of violence. Walker's words also encouraged more blacks to take up the cause of abolitionism. Even as Walker had an impact on those who supported abolition, he also influenced those who were against it. Such dramatic and angry language spread fear among whites in the South.

The impact of Nat Turner on Garrison occurred in a completely different way but was probably even more profound. In the late summer of 1831, the residents of southeastern Virginia experienced a slave uprising led by Nat Turner, a slave and part-time preacher. It came about after Turner claimed he had received a "sign from heaven."[58] He became convinced that he had been chosen by God to lead a slave revolt. Turner claimed to have experienced dreams and visions, including "blood on the corn and strange human figures in the air."[59] "I saw white spirits and black spirits engaged in battle," he said, "and the sun darkened—thunder rolled in the heavens, and blood flowed in the streams."[60] He convinced 70 or so slaves to join him. Turner and his followers rampaged through Southampton County and "within twenty-four hours, almost all the men, women, and children of what had been a quiet, rural area a few miles from the county seat, Jerusalem, to the number of fifty-seven, had been slaughtered."[61] Whites, including militia forces, rose up to quell the revolt. Turner and 17 of his followers were tried a few months later, were found guilty of insurrection against the state and of treason, and were hanged. In a show of fear and revenge, whites in both Virginia and North Carolina killed approximately 100 blacks they suspected (although they were often wrong) were part of the Turner uprising.

The writings of David Walker and the insurrection of Nat Turner each played a role in hardening William Lloyd Garrison's message against slavery. They had another impact as well. The Turner-inspired killings in Virginia sickened many Southerners, even as they were angered. Much of the abolitionist movement and reform work in the South dried up after the Turner revolt. Although these factors did not completely eliminate antislavery sentiment in the South, "they combined to give it a blow from which it could never recover, and they were all but fatal to the organized expressions of antislavery sentiment."[62] Whites feared new slave revolts. The movement to abolish slavery became, almost overnight and almost exclusively, a Northern campaign by the early 1830s.

I WILL BE HEARD!

On New Year's Day, 1831, William Lloyd Garrison took a bold step that would irrevocably change his campaign against slavery. He launched a new antislavery paper he aptly called *The Liberator*. It would continue to be published for the next 35 years. Garrison wasted no time or editorial space in explaining his intent and purpose. His first issue threw down the gauntlet:

> In Park Street Church, on the Fourth of July, 1829, in an address on slavery, I [thoughtlessly agreed] to the popular but pernicious doctrine of *gradual* abolition. I seize this opportunity to make a full . . . recantation.
>
> I will be as harsh as truth, and as uncompromising as justice. On this subject I do not wish to think, or to speak or write, with moderation. No! No! Tell a man whose house is on fire to give a moderate alarm . . . but [do not] urge me . . . to use moderation in a cause like the present. I am in earnest—I will not equivocate—I will not excuse—I will not retreat a single inch—and I WILL BE HEARD.[63]

He addressed blacks who lived under the yoke of slavery and asked for their support, stating his awareness "that you are now struggling against wind and tide."[64]

Garrison's new paper represented a more militant view of how slavery should end and when. The change was a recognition that the decades of campaigns on behalf of gradualism had not put a dent in the institution of

..I.]   WILLIAM LLOYD GARRISON AND ISAAC KNAPP, PUBLISHERS.   [NO. 22
ION, MASSACHUSETTS.]   OUR COUNTRY IS THE WORLD—OUR COUNTRYMEN ARE MANKIND.   [SATURDAY, MAY 28, 1831.

In 1831, abolitionist William Lloyd Garrison launched *The Liberator,* one of the nation's first antislavery newspapers. Although it took awhile for Garrison's paper to become successful, the paper eventually had a readership of 3,000, three-quarters of whom were African Americans.

slavery. The policy of calm insistence that slavery should be eliminated had failed. Not only was slavery no closer to ending, but it also had expanded across the country into Kentucky, Florida, Tennessee, Alabama, Mississippi, Louisiana, Missouri, Arkansas, and Texas. In 1800, the slave population in the United States had stood at close to 900,000. Each decade, the number had increased: 1.5 million by 1820 and 2 million by 1830.

His start with his new paper had been awkward. Garrison had needed help, for he had no money, printing office, or printing press of his own. A young Bostonian lawyer named Samuel Sewall had provided the necessary funds. With help from Sewall and others, Garrison was finally able to print his paper. His first folio issue was only four pages and measured 14 × 9¼ inches. It was printed in boldface type. A yearlong subscription was $2. As the first issues of the paper came off the presses, the newly dedicated Bostonian abolitionist was just 25 years old.

Garrison was not immediately heard, however. The early issues of *The Liberator* did not raise any new interest or

A LEADING VOICE

William Lloyd Garrison rose to prominence in the United States from a humble beginning. Born in 1805, he was the "son of a demoralized sailor who deserted his family in 1808."[*] Young William grew up in poverty in Newburyport, Massachusetts, in the household of his mother, a strongly religious Baptist. While he was still young, his mother moved to Baltimore, where she tried to apprentice him first as a shoemaker and then as a cabinetmaker, but he rejected both trades. By age 13, he was apprenticed to learn the printing trade in the offices of the *Newburyport Herald*. Over the next seven years, he gained valuable practical experience and worked on his skills as a writer. By age 20, he was completely trained, and Garrison set out to make his way in the world. He was reasonably good looking (but a bit nearsighted) and was a proper, neatly dressed young man who was "sober, industrious, [and] religious." Garrison also seems to have been "quite popular with the ladies."[**]

For a few years, Garrison struggled with himself, uncertain of what to do with his life. Always a bit idealistic, he thought he might go to Europe and aid the Greeks in their struggle to gain independence from the Turks. He considered a military career, which would start with attendance at the United States Military Academy. He yearned to do something important, to make a bold statement. By 1826, he went into business with another Newburyport printer, Isaac Knapp, but their paper, the *Free Press,* did not last through the year. From there, he went to Boston, where he found other opportunities. Soon, he was writing for a reform newspaper, the first temperance publication, the *National Philanthropist,* published by Reverend William Collier. By January 1828, Garrison had worked his way up to editor. Through these years, Garrison was interested in the various reform movements that were taking place in the United States. He became familiar with other reform publications, including Lundy's the *Genius of Universal Emancipation.*

---

[*] Louis Filler, *The Crusade Against Slavery, 1830–1860* (New York: Harper & Row, 1960), 56.
[**] Ibid.

controversy in Boston or anywhere else. Issues did not sell well, and the public appeared somewhat apathetic. He found it difficult to pay his printing costs. Having set up shop in Boston's Merchants' Hall, he moved from Number 6 to 8 to 19 to 11; the last one was the cheapest to rent. He stayed his course, though, and, with the help of his associate, fellow printer Isaac Knapp, Garrison worked 14-hour days in an editorial office that was "furnished with two chairs, a desk, and a table on which Garrison often slept. A cake and fruit shop in the basement provided minimum rations."[65]

William Lloyd Garrison was so intent on redefining the antislavery cause that his readers, many of whom were free African Americans, could have no doubts of his intent. Garrison's words speak for themselves: "If we would not see our land deluged in blood, we must instantly burst asunder the shackles of the slaves."[66] His black readers could not help but appreciate Garrison's twofold goal for his newspaper, which included not only "immediatism" but also racial equality for all blacks in the United States. Garrison believed these two goals went hand in hand. If American slaveholders wanted to avoid wholesale uprisings and miscellaneous violence against themselves and others, they would have to free their slaves and give them rights equal to those of any white man in the country.

OTHER OPPONENTS OF SLAVERY

Garrison did not have to stand alone against the evils of slavery. He had close associates, like-minded people who were part of his always-small, but ever-increasing, group of brothers in the cause of abolitionism. One of his closest comrades was Wendell Phillips, a highly skilled speaker sometimes called by admirers the "Golden Trumpet of Abolitionism," as well as the "Knight-Errant of Unfriended Truth." Phillips took his opposition to slavery so seriously that he would not allow either sugar or cotton in his house, because they were both products of slavery.

The abolitionist cause, then, gained a new focus and emphasis through William Lloyd Garrison and his personal views. Abolitionists began to campaign for equality for blacks just as fervently as they called for slavery to end. Both slavery and the laws that denied free blacks their equal rights would have to be eradicated. One abolitionist, Lydia Maria Child, described these laws as nothing more than a "legalized contempt of color."[67] Such laws were, unfortunately, on the books in every state in the Union. Differences existed between the states in this regard, of course. New England states, for example, allowed free blacks to vote. The laws in general, though, segregated blacks in the use of a variety of public facilities. They also denied blacks the right to migrate into several states in the West. Opportunities were few and limited for America's blacks, even those who were freemen. They were permitted to take only jobs that required no real skill. These restrictions placed on America's blacks a badge of inferiority.

Garrison did have a solid core of supporters, both black and white, in Boston, throughout New England, and beyond. Garrison's fervent message—that slavery must be abolished immediately—would not fall on deaf ears. His concept of immediatism soon found converts in New York City, upstate New York, Pennsylvania, and Ohio, in addition to New England. Supporters grew in number, and they, too, came to believe that slavery was morally wrong and that they must fight for emancipation. Some of those who took up the cause as their own were inspired by a wave of religious revivalism that had been sweeping the United States, especially the North, during the late 1820s. Fired with religious zeal, they viewed slavery as one of the greatest sins of man against man. These converts to

In 1833, William Lloyd Garrison (depicted here) and Arthur Tappan founded the American Anti-Slavery Society. Within two years of its founding, the society had more than 150,000 members in 1,000 local chapters throughout the country.

immediatism "called on all Americans to recognize their Christian duty to end a system of human bondage that deprived the enslaved of their God-given right to be free moral beings."[68]

ORGANIZING BEHIND THE CAUSE

Even though William Lloyd Garrison's voice began to be heard across the United States, he was only one voice; only one man. Although others supported him in their protest of laws that denied blacks their freedom and in their passionate writing about the wrongness of slavery, there was a need for abolitionists to work together and in tandem as much as possible. This meant that the movement needed to organize itself on a national scale. Without such an umbrella organization, the words of Garrison and his supporters might not be heard outside black communities across the North. In 1832, he and others formed the New England Anti-Slavery Society in Boston in the city's first black church, the African Meeting House. The society was open to both black and white members, and it joined with another group, the Massachusetts General Colored Association, which was founded in 1826.

American abolitionists could look across the Atlantic for one of the best examples of how to successfully organize against slavery. In 1833, British antislavery advocates banded together and helped bring about legal changes that called for gradual emancipation in Great Britain's slave colonies in the Caribbean. This action was enough to inspire American abolitionists to meet, again with Garrison's help, in Philadelphia in December 1833 and organize the American Anti-Slavery Society (AASS). The organization received much of its financial backing from two wealthy New York businessmen and brothers, Arthur and Lewis Tappan, who were already members of several reform societies in New York. The AASS counted important black members among its ranks. The society hosted some of the most inspiring black voices of its time, including those of Frederick Douglass, Sojourner Truth, and William Wells Brown, and they helped to recruit new members and broaden the society's appeal. Antislavery societies for children also sprang up; an example was Boston's Juvenile Garrison

(continues on page 70)

THE SENECA FALLS CONVENTION

Today, women in the United States expect to be treated as citizens equal to men. Federal and state laws have been passed throughout the twentieth century in support of that expectation. Women, however, have not always had their rights recognized and guaranteed. Various women's rights movements and organized groups have campaigned through the years to gain everything for women from equal pay for equal work to the vote. During the 1830s and 1840s, women took up the cause of reform to improve their place in the United States.

During the first half of the nineteenth century, women were treated as second-class citizens. They had few recognized rights, and most of those were granted by individual states, not the national government. To gain the rights that women knew they deserved, a reform movement on their behalf took root, one that paralleled the campaign against slavery. As one abolitionist Quaker woman argued, "In striving to cut [the slave's] irons off, we found most surely that we were manacled ourselves."[*]

Sometimes, then, women in the United States supported both the women's rights movement and the fight for abolition. Two sisters from South Carolina serve as good examples. In 1837, Angelina and Sarah Grimké took up the cause of abolition and engaged in a speaking tour in New England. Even though their cause was noble and New England a part of the country where abolitionism thrived, the Grimkés were immediately criticized. Many of their critics were Congregational ministers who were scandalized that the sisters were speaking to mixed audiences of men and women. For women to lecture men was virtually unheard of at that time in America. The Grimké sisters resisted their critics and spoke against those men who tried to silence them, stating publicly that men and women should be considered equal. They argued that "whatever is right for man to do is right for woman."[**]

Following their example, women within the abolitionist movement began to call for a voice equal to that of men in the movement. This call proved extremely unpopular with the men. Garrison, however, was not among them. In 1840, he supported the women's cause and helped a woman, Abby Kelley, to be seated on an important committee of the AASS. This bold step led a large group of anti-Garrisonians to walk out of the society's annual convention. In opposition, these renegades formed a separate abolitionist group, the American and Foreign Anti-Slavery Society.

Women within the abolitionist movement continued their struggle for equality. That same year, at the convention of the World Anti-Slavery Convention in London, some American female delegates were not allowed to take their seats. Two of those women excluded from the convention were Lucretia Mott and Elizabeth Cady Stanton. Outraged at their treatment, they returned to the United States and soon formed a new movement on behalf of women's rights and equality.

In many ways, their movement resembled the antislavery movement in the United States. The movement's roots, after all, had sprung from the abolitionist movement. They held meetings, wrote political and social tracts, and engaged in speaking tours. They even held a national convention. In 1848, both Mott and Stanton organized the first national meeting on behalf of women's rights. The delegates met in upstate New York at Seneca Falls. The result was an important document called the Declaration of Sentiments. The document called for full and equal rights for women, and it was patterned after the Declaration of Independence. The women at the convention had written a statement in support of women's rights that included the right to full citizenship and access to the vote.

The women's rights campaign and movement did not engender a great deal of support, however. Its sister movement, abolitionism, managed to help bring about the end of American slavery by the 1860s. As for the women's movement, although women gradually won rights over many decades, they did not even gain the right to vote nationally until the 1920s. Former slaves, by comparison, had received the right to vote nearly a half century earlier.

---

* David Goldfield, *The American Journey: A History of the United States* (Upper Saddle River, N.J.: Pearson Education, 2007), 363.
** Ibid.

(continued from page 67)
Independent Society, which formed around a performing group that sang at abolitionist rallies.

The 1830s witnessed the first steps taken by the AASS. During those early years, the AASS hammered out a platform and philosophy centered on the assumption of moral suasion (today, the more common term is *persuasion*). The call went out for Americans, in both the North and the South, to join in support of abolitionism and equal rights. Many of the organization's statements rang especially true to those individuals who were Christian. The AASS described slavery as a sin on the heads of those who practiced it. The act of slaveholding itself was evil, but also those who practiced it sometimes abused their slaves physically or sexually. Both sins required God's forgiveness. Members of the society admonished slaveholders to give up their sin, free their slaves, and fight to free the slaves of others. Only by doing so would good Christians be able to save themselves from God's wrath and his damnation.

Other arguments were advanced by those who aligned themselves with the AASS. They wrote and spoke of the economic aspects of slavery and of how the institution was "an inefficient labor system that enriched a few masters but impoverished most black and white southerners and hurt the economy of the United States as a whole."[69]

CRITICS OF IMMEDIATISM

When Garrison and others embraced immediatism concerning slavery, their beliefs were not always accepted. By the mid-1830s, abolitionists began a blitz of the American postal system with a propaganda campaign of letters, pamphlets, and other documents. Printing presses of the era were capable of massive output, and the abolitionists put out "a million pieces of antislavery literature," the vast majority of which found their way across the South.[70] With Nat Turner's slave revolt still fresh in their minds, many Southerners were aghast at the content of the unsolicited abolitionist literature and feared such language would incite new slave revolts. Rallies were held, and abolitionist materials were burned in great bonfires. Some Southerners appealed to the federal mail system, requesting that such inflammatory materials be banned from being circulated. President Andrew Jackson agreed to do so.

With the South successful in its attempt to stop the delivery of this unwanted antislavery material, the abolitionists stepped up their efforts and focused on another campaign, one that targeted the U.S. Congress. If slavery existed under and because of U.S. law, then antislavery supporters would try to have those laws stricken from the books. This campaign began in earnest in 1836 and would continue throughout Martin Van Buren's presidency. (Van Buren had been Jackson's second vice president and was elected president in 1836.) The halls of Congress were regularly flooded with "hundreds of thousands of antislavery petitions, some with thousands of signatures."[71] The majority of these petitions demanded the abolition of slavery within the District of Columbia, the capital of the U.S. government. To many, it seemed ironic that slavery and slave trading existed within sight of the seat of American democracy. Southern congressmen did not appreciate such literature on their desks any more than many Southerners liked receiving theirs in the mail. A countercampaign was launched, with Southern legislators "demanding that free speech be repressed in the name of southern white security."[72] Such infamous materials, Southern leaders insisted, were the product of wild-eyed, antislavery fanaticism. As one congressman from South Carolina, Francis Pickens, argued, they must "meet it and strangle it in its infancy."[73] The result was a gag rule placed on the U.S. Congress. This movement blocked all such abolitionist petitions from being presented in either house. These petitions would simply be tabled, and no discussion would be allowed. This gag rule would remain in effect for eight years, from 1836 until 1844, during the terms of three different presidents.

Such political moves, even when made by the U.S. Congress, did not deter Garrison and other abolitionists from their goals. In 1838, Garrison and others established the New England Non-Resistant Society. The group's purpose centered on "the belief that a complete moral regeneration, based on renouncing force in all human relationships, was necessary if America was ever to live up to its Christian and republican ideals."[74] The end result of this view is somewhat less clear than the society's mission statement. The view of the society's members was that all coercive authority was wrong. This view would include everything from the person who owned slaves against their will; to husbands who, as authority figures, mistreated their spouses; and even to the power of the government. In the end, the group's inherent "Christian anarchy" led its members to believe that the power of the U.S. government was wrong and that the society's members should steer clear of all political activity. In part, it was the upheld legality of slavery that drove Garrison and his fellow society members to question the legitimacy of the American Union. This stance caused Garrison to burn a copy of the U.S. Constitution and claim that it represented a "covenant with death and an agreement with Hell."[75]

6

Politics of Abolitionism

Although such steps as burning the U.S. Constitution represented bold statements in opposition to slavery, they also gave Garrison's opponents, some of whom were in the abolitionist movement itself, ammunition. They claimed that he was hurting the antislavery cause by the assumption of extreme positions and actions. He could gain little, they argued, by the complete alienation of patriotic Americans. The result of such antagonistic positions by Garrison represented a split that developed within the abolitionist movement. (Another controversial position taken by Garrison was that regarding women. He began to speak out in support of many of the women within the movement who wanted to be considered equals with men.) In time, factional disagreement among abolitionists produced a parting of the ways between groups within the AASS. Simultaneously, a group of women abolitionists began to establish a separate reform movement of their own. This activity would develop into a splinter group of reformers who would intently campaign on behalf of women's rights.

BREAKING AWAY FROM GARRISON

Garrison's harsh indictment of the American political system did not stop some abolitionists from continued involvement in politics and elections. They believed the best way to bring about important change and advance the antislavery cause was through politics. Such political involvement dated from the 1830s. During those years, hundreds of thousands of abolition supporters drafted and signed petitions in opposition to the gag rule that was in place in Congress. They also voiced their hope that Texas would not be allowed to join the Union as a slave state. (In this, they ultimately failed, as Texas became a slave state in 1845.)

By 1840, abolitionists defied Garrison's call to steer clear of the evils of the American political system and formed a new political party. Since neither the Democrats nor the Whigs (this political party would barely survive the 1840s intact) would support the cause of abolition, a third party was necessary. It was called the Liberty Party, and its candidate was a former slaveholder named James G. Birney, who had been converted by Theodore Weld to the cause of abolition. The party's stance centered on opposition to the expansion of slavery into America's western territories and on condemnation of slavery and racial discrimination. Many black abolitionists supported the Liberty Party.

Abolitionism, however, was a fringe movement in the United States, and many voters could not cast their vote in support of an antislavery presidential candidate. Birney did not manage to garner even one vote of every 100. Despite his failure, the Liberty Party did elect a handful of abolitionist candidates from New England to the U.S. Congress, as well as New Yorker Gerrit Smith.

During the early 1840s, the Liberty Party continued the struggle against slavery and kept the issue front and center in American politics. Members of the party followed the leadership of party member Joshua R. Giddings. The party's small number of members continued to voice their opposition to what they called "the Slave Power."[76] This term was defined as a large conspiracy of Southern politicians and planters who had the ear of sympathetic Northerners and who, between them, controlled national politics and the power of the national government.

Those who represented the Slave Power worked tirelessly, sometimes secretly, to spread the scope and influence of slavery. To do so, they often caused problems for free institutions and groups who opposed their slave-supporting agenda. Liberty Party members offered proof of this vast proslavery political conspiracy in the gag rule that had been in effect in Congress for eight years, as well as President Tyler's campaign to bring Texas into the Union as a slave state as quickly as possible. In 1843, Liberty Party supporters in Michigan described slavery as "not only a monstrous legalized system of wickedness . . . but an overwhelming political monopoly . . . which has thus tyrannically subverted the constitutional liberties of more than 12,000,000 of nominal American freemen."[77]

When the United States experienced a severe depression between 1839 and 1843, Liberty Party advocates blamed it on the "withering and impoverishing effect of slavery on the free states."[78] Southern landowners had defaulted on the debts they owed to Northern banking and finance houses and had manipulated national banking and tariff policies to their own advantage. The claim by Liberty Party backers of a Slave Power conspiracy, with its hands in the pockets of Northerners, made inroads into American public opinion. Slavery was ultimately seen as an evil foisted on unsuspecting Northern whites.

Despite its small membership, the Liberty Party continued as a voice of opposition to slavery. James G. Birney ran as the party's candidate again in 1844 but performed only slightly better at the polls than he had four years earlier. The Slave Power theory continued to gain support and legitimacy. When a Southern Democrat, James K. Polk, won the presidency that year, some Northerners were suspicious of his campaign promises to annex Texas, as well as the region of the Pacific Northwest, known then as Oregon Country, to the United States. Was he, as some thought, merely gaining more territory for the federal government so that slavery could spread far beyond the American South?

OTHER MEANS, OTHER VOICES

The Liberty Party was just one way in which anti-Garrison abolitionists took up a new form of opposition to slavery. The party was supported by black abolitionists, who were themselves making inroads on behalf of the antislavery movement. One such black campaigner was a former slave— Frederick Douglass. He was the son of an unknown white man and a slave mother. Douglass had escaped slavery as a young man in 1838. He became one of the most important black abolitionists of his day and campaigned against the evils of slavery for nearly the next 30 years. He lectured on slavery and abolitionism. Before curious crowds, Douglass would relate his past as a slave: "I appear this evening as a thief and a robber," he would say. "I stole this head, these limbs, this body from my master, and ran off with them."[79] In 1845, he published his autobiography, which graphically told his personal story of escape from slavery, titled *Narrative of the Life of Frederick Douglass, an American Slave.* (William Lloyd Garrison wrote the book's preface, which he ended with the following words: "NO COMPROMISE WITH SLAVERY! NO UNION WITH SLAVEHOLDERS!")[80]

In his book, Douglass describes his experiences with both a cruel overseer and a harsh master:

> I have had two masters. My first master's name was Anthony. I do not remember his first name. . . . His farms were under the care of an overseer. The overseer's name was Plummer. Mr. Plummer was a miserable drunkard, a profane swearer, and a savage monster. He always went

Frederick Douglass, who is depicted in this circa 1850 daguerreotype, was the son of a unknown white man and slave mother. He escaped slavery in 1838 and eventually made his way to Massachusetts, where he quickly developed a friendship with William Lloyd Garrison.

armed with a cowskin [leather whip] and a heavy cudgel. I have known him to cut and slash the women's heads so horribly, that even master would be enraged at his cruelty, and would threaten to whip him if he did not mind himself. Master, however, was not a humane slaveholder. . . . He was a cruel man, hardened by a long life of slaveholding. He would at times seem to take great pleasure in whipping a slave. I have often been awakened at the dawn of day by the most heart-rending shrieks of an own aunt of mine, whom he used to tie up to a joist, and whip upon the naked back till she was literally covered with blood. No words, no tears, no prayers, from his gory victim, seemed to move his iron heart from its bloody purpose. The louder she screamed, the harder he whipped; and where the blood ran fastest, there he whipped longest. He would whip her to make her scream, and whip her to make her hush; and not until overcome by fatigue, would he cease to swing the blood-clotted cowskin.[81]

Although Douglass was associated with William Lloyd Garrison for several years, he eventually became disappointed with Garrison's "Christian pacifism and his stand against political action."[82] He parted political company with Garrison and founded his own black abolitionist newspaper, the *North Star*, in 1847 (see sidebar on pages 79–80). One important sticking point between the two men was Garrison's view of the U.S. Constitution. Garrison believed it was a document that supported slavery in spirit. Douglass interpreted it differently, insisting "the Constitution is a glorious liberty document."[83]

Few speakers inspired their audiences as did Frederick Douglass. He was "tall, handsome, and strongly built, standing in front of an audience recounting his heart-rending tales of bondage and his longing for freedom."[84] The women's reformer Elizabeth Cady Stanton described the impact Douglass could have on an audience:

He stood there like an African prince, majestic in his wrath, as with wit, satire and indignation he graphically described the bitterness of slavery and the humiliation of subjection to those who were . . . inferior to himself. Thus it was that I first saw Frederick Douglass, and wondered that any mortal man should have ever tried to subjugate a being with such talents, intensified with the love of liberty.[85]

IMPACT OF BLACK NEWSPAPERS

Although such abolitionist newspapers as William Lloyd Garrison's *The Liberator* were among the most influential publications of the antislavery movement, other voices against slavery made their way into print as well. A significant number of newspapers were written and published by whites, but blacks did publish similar ones.

Many of these black papers first appeared between the time the American Anti-Slavery Society (AASS) was established in 1833 and the start of the Civil War nearly 30 years later. One, called *Freedom's Journal,* first came into print in 1827. It was owned and published by two black businessmen, Samuel Cornish and John B. Russwurm. In its pages, Cornish and Russwurm emphasized the abolitionist cause, fought for racial equality, and put forward their support for Christian ideals and democratic values. Their paper was also opposed to the "back to Africa" colonization movement. The paper attracted both black and white subscribers.

Another important black abolitionist newspaper publisher was Philip A. Bell. Bell published two abolitionist papers. The first was New York City's *Weekly Advocate,* which began in 1837. The paper's name was changed later that same year to the *Colored American.* (It was important to Bell that the word *American* be used in his paper's name. "We are Americans," he explained, "colored Americans."*)

To produce his papers, Bell relied on other black professionals, such as Charles B. Ray, a minister from New York. Ray was a man of God, editor, and businessman all wrapped into one. He was keenly aware of the financial difficulties that plagued most abolitionist presses in the United States. He wrote in 1838: "If among the few hundred thousand free colored people in the country—to say nothing of the white population from whom it ought to receive a strong support—a living patronage for the paper cannot be obtained, it will be greatly to their reproach."**

Other such papers were produced during the 1840s and 1850s on the presses of black supporters, editors, and writers. They included Henry Highland Garnet's *Clarion*, Stephen Myers's *Northern Star* and *Freeman's Advocate,*

(continues)

(continued)

Samuel Ringgold Ward's *True American* (it was later re-named the *Impartial American*), and Thomas Van Rens-selaer's *Ram's Horn*, all of which were published in New York State. In Pittsburgh, Martin Delany published his black abolitionist paper, the *Mystery*, during the 1840s.

One American black newspaper publisher stood out above the others during the decades preceding the Civil War. Among the most famous black men of the nineteenth century, Frederick Douglass published two extremely important newspapers, both dedicated to the cause of antislavery—first *North Star* and then *Frederick Douglass' Paper.* Douglass's papers were published beginning in the late 1840s and early 1850s. After they became established, they were backed primarily by a white abolitionist businessman, Gerrit Smith. Whereas white-published abolitionist papers often attracted readers from the community of free blacks, Douglass's papers were read by blacks and whites alike. Douglass's papers were highly professional publications, well crafted, edited, and printed. Douglass's papers, however, were not established on the support of American abolitionists. Most of the funds needed to begin publication of *North Star* were donated by antislavery advocates in Great Britain.

---

* James Oliver Horton and Lois E. Horton, *Slavery and the Making of America* (New York: Oxford University Press, 2005), 97.
** Darlene Clark Hine, *The African-American Odyssey* (Upper Saddle River, N.J.: Prentice Hall, 2005), 196–197.

UNDERGROUND RAILROAD

Although the vast majority of America's slaves during the nineteenth century chose to remain slaves and refused to give in to the lure of escape to safety in the North, some could not remain confined by the institution. To leave the harsh reality of a difficult master and safely reach the Northern United States, and then, perhaps, Canada, not only was a difficult decision but also difficult to accomplish. By the 1830s, the famous escape route for

Fugitive slaves used the Underground Railroad to escape to the free states of the North and Canada. Pictured here is a stop along the Underground Railroad in the basement of Joseph Hurlbutt's house in Wilton, Connecticut.

slaves was in place and provided a series of safe places for them to stay while they covered hundreds of miles of Southern territory before they set foot in the North. That escape route and system of safe places came to be known as the Underground Railroad.

It was a fitting name, even if no one really knows how it first came to be used. Railroads were new to the United States but were expanding across the country, both in the North and in the South. With regard to the Underground Railroad, the various stations along the way were occupied and run by abolitionists and other slavery opponents, and its various routes included ships secretly launched from the harbor at Charleston, South Carolina, to a far western route that ran from western Missouri into the unorganized Kansas

Territory and then north across a corner of Nebraska to the safety of the free state of Iowa.

Much of the earliest work of the Underground Railroad was begun, it seems, during the 1830s. The "railroad" system was actually a series of separate escape routes, not "a united national underground railroad with a president or unified command."[86]

All along the Underground Railroad routes, secrecy was the watchword. The "system required a series of safeguards for fugitives bound for freedom, and catchphrases and secret rappings were abundant. The use of the call of a hoot owl was a popular sign in the west of Virginia."[87] It was all necessarily elaborate, well organized, and built on the railroad lingo of the day:

> The members of this secret network used code words and spoke of themselves as "agents" of the UGRR [Underground Railroad]. Some were "stationmasters" at "stations" or "depots" [safe houses] where "conductors" [UGRR escorts] and their "cargo" [fugitives] might rest before resuming their journey on the "liberty lines" [paths where escorted fugitives were smuggled north]. When they corresponded with one another, they might use other kinds of subterfuge, as when Delaware stationmaster Thomas Garrett wrote, "I sent you three bales of black wool" [three fugitives].[88]

Some of the most important connections and best-organized legs of the Underground Railroad were located in Washington, D.C., and Ripley, Ohio, where Reverend Rankin lived. By the early 1840s, two abolitionists, Charles T. Torrey, a white man who was involved with the Liberty Party, and a free black named Thomas Smallwood, were directly involved in the efforts to help slaves make their way to freedom through the District of Columbia. During 1842 alone, these two antislavery men helped approximately 150 escaped slaves reach the North. Typically, those who passed through the nation's capital were whisked northward to Albany, New York, and then on to Canada. At each stage in the escape beyond Washington, D.C., vigilance groups guided black escapees from station to station. The Washington–Albany line became one of the most widely used lines of the Underground Railroad. By the establishment of a connection between these two important cities, it was a line "radiating in all directions to all the New England States and to many parts of [New York] state."[89]

In Ripley, located in southern Ohio on the Ohio River, black and white abolitionist conductors helped fugitive slaves who escaped across the river from Kentucky. Among the most important abolitionists in Ripley was a former slave named John P. Parker. He and Reverend Rankin worked closely together. Parker made forays into Kentucky to guide slaves out, in the same manner as Harriet Tubman. One of the most famous of the Underground Railroad conductors, Tubman was an escaped slave herself who began to guide slaves out of bondage to freedom by the early 1850s. She would later describe how her decision to work as a conductor for the Underground Railroad took place. "The Lord told me to do this," she claimed. "I said, 'Oh Lord, I can't—don't ask me—take somebody else.'" She stated that she heard God speak to her directly and thus emphasized that the choice was not hers: "It's you I want, Harriet Tubman."[90]

Harriet Tubman was born in 1820 on a plantation in Maryland. She was mistreated by her master but never considered escape a serious option until she faced the threat that she and her family were to be "sold south," a common term in the slave world that often meant harsher treatment in the Deep South. (Two of her sisters had already been sold south.) In 1849, Tubman escaped from her plantation on the Eastern Shore of Maryland and received help from kindly

Known as the "Moses of her people," Harriet Tubman escaped slavery in 1849 and moved to Philadelphia. From there she worked closely with the Underground Railroad and made 19 trips to the South to help free slaves.

abolitionists along the way, until she reached Philadelphia. This Pennsylvania city was one of the other important destinations on the Underground Railroad, and the black abolitionist William Still directed the activities of the local vigilance committee. In the years that followed, Tubman worked closely with Still.

In a few short years, after repeated returns to the South and the guidance of escaped slaves to the North, Tubman became notorious across the Upper South. There was a reward for her capture. Tubman remained committed to the goal of freedom for slaves, however. During the decade before the Civil War, Harriet Tubman risked her life and liberty as a worker on the Underground Railroad. She became known for "her daring rescues, complicated plans, and determination."[91] Stories told of how she led her escapees down back roads while she sang spirituals such as "Steal Away" or "Bound for the Promised Land." Her admirers soon referred to her as "Black Moses."

Clash of Regions

Nearly from the time the United States became a nation, questions had arisen not just about whether slavery should exist but also about whether it should be allowed to expand into new American regions, especially into the western territories. By the 1850s, this question loomed larger in the minds of Americans, both Northerners and Southerners, than ever before. The 1840s had witnessed the annexation of Texas as a slave state and the Oregon Country as a vast territory that included the modern states of Washington, Oregon, and Idaho. Between 1846 and 1848, the United States fought and won a war against Mexico (the army was led by two Southern generals, Winfield Scott and Zachary Taylor, and two of every three soldiers were Southerners). The war resulted in a large grant of land to the United States that extended from California to Texas, a massive annexation that added 1.25 million square miles to the young republic. Of that land, approximately half of it was below the 36°30' parallel established under the Missouri Compromise. When gold was discovered in California in the late 1840s, so many Americans rushed out to stake their claims in the search for riches that the population in the region became large enough to form a new American territory. Suddenly, within a few short years, the territory of the United States included land from the Gulf of Mexico to the Gulf of California, from the northern Rockies to the Pacific Northwest. With all this new land, the issue of slavery and where it would exist next became an extremely volatile issue.

SLAVERY AND THE WEST

In 1850, events in California gained the attention of the nation. Americans there wanted their territory to enter the Union as a free state. Southerners objected. Once again, Henry Clay, who was now a senator, advanced an agreement designed to appease both sides on the issue.

California would become a free state. In exchange for this concession and to mollify Southerners, Congress passed a stricter fugitive slave law. It replaced legislation that was more than a half century old, the Fugitive Slave Act of 1793.

There was, though, an important difference between the two. The earlier law had authorized Northern law enforcement officials, such as city policemen and town sheriffs, to aid Southerners in the capture of escaped slaves who had made it to freedom in the North. The law did not require such cooperation, however, and most Northern states had, over the years, passed personal liberty laws that typically forbade their officials from assistance with the recapture of escaped slaves. Even after the U.S. Supreme Court decided, in the 1842 case *Prigg v. Pennsylvania*, that the Fugitive Slave Act of 1793 brought into question state laws that tried to protect escaped slaves by the guarantee of a trial by jury, states passed even more such laws. Now, under the Fugitive Slave Act of 1850, "federal agents were ordered to assist in the seizure of runaways, and ordinary citizens who helped a slave escape were subject to a fine of $2,000 and six months in jail."[92] Once again, Clay had steered the country clear of a

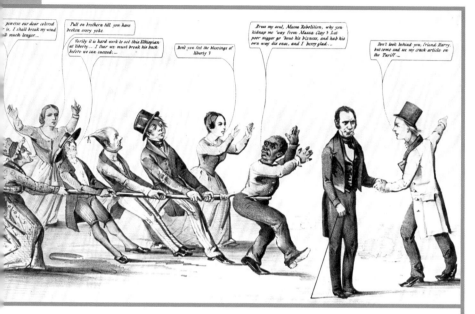

In this 1851 cartoon titled "The Blessings of Liberty or How to Hook a Gentleman of Color," an unwilling black man is being pulled toward a diverse group of abolitionists, as Henry Clay and Horace Greeley converse on the right. Clay and Greeley represent freedom, while the abolitionists are attempting to indoctrinate the black man in their ways before he can gain the freedom he desires.

break between the North and South. Massachusetts senator Daniel Webster lauded the agreement: "The Union stands firm,"[93] he said.

The law struck a chord across the North. President Franklin Pierce insisted the new law be obeyed. He had his critics, however. "Let the President drench our land of freedom in blood," cried Joshua Giddings, an abolitionist congressman from Ohio, "but he will never make us obey *that* law."[94] Abolitionists were not the only ones stirred with anger by the federal mandate. The city council of Chicago passed a resolution against the Fugitive Slave Act, calling it a "violation of both the Constitution and the laws of God."[95] In towns across the North, rallies against the act were held, church bells tolled in protest, and American flags were hung at half-mast. Two years later, in a speech at a Fourth of July celebration in Rochester, New York, where the majority of the crowd was white, Frederick Douglass lashed out against the new fugitive slave law:

> Are the great principles of political freedom and of natural justice, embodied in [the] Declaration of Independence, extended to us? This Fourth of July is yours not mine. You may rejoice, I must mourn. To drag a man in fetters into the grand illuminated temple of liberty, and call upon him to join you in joyous anthems, were inhuman mockery and sacrilegious irony.[96]

After a fugitive slave named Anthony Burns was captured in Boston in 1854 and ordered to be returned to the South by the federal court, riots broke out in the city, and federal troops were called in to stop the violence. The Burns case made converts of a large number of Northerners who had never considered opposing slavery. In the words of one Bostonian, "We went to bed one night old-fashioned, conservative Compromise Union Whigs and waked up stark mad abolitionists."[97]

Beyond the obvious, the Fugitive Slave Act of 1850 had an immediate impact on free blacks in the North. Many of those who had only recently escaped slavery chose to move to Canada to ensure their safety and continued freedom. Other blacks who had escaped even decades earlier elected to do the same. Most of these new refugees lived in towns and villages close to a Southern slave state, which made them more vulnerable to recapture. In Columbia, Pennsylvania, the black population dropped by half. In Pittsburgh, "nearly all the waiters in the hotels fled to Canada."[98] Even in towns that already bordered Canada, such as Buffalo, New York, blacks packed up and migrated across the border. One black church in the city lost 130 parishioners. In Rochester, New York, membership in the city's black Baptist church dropped from 114 to just 2. Other churches, in New York, Boston, and Albany, also experienced a decline, all from fear of the new fugitive slave law. During the decade between 1850 and 1860, as many as 20,000 American blacks who lived in the assumed safety of the North left the country for Canada.

LIFE AMONG THE LOWLY

Just as the Fugitive Slave Act of 1850 created a stir of controversy in the abolitionist arena, so did the publication of a novel two years later. Its author was the aforementioned Harriet Beecher Stowe, the daughter of Lyman Beecher, a minister and one of New England's most influential abolitionists. When Harriet Beecher was a young girl, her father had moved his family from New England to Ohio, where he took over the leadership of the Lane Theological Seminary. There, he and other faculty members had taught their ministerial students about the evils of slavery. All six of Harriet Beecher Stowe's brothers became Christian ministers. For most of his adult life, Lyman Beecher believed and taught that "evangelical Christianity erased the line between public and private."[99] This view led him to believe that a single person's salvation and that of the general society as a whole were linked. He who opposes slavery, he would teach, must campaign for society to take the same moral view. Harriet Beecher Stowe would adopt that same position. Although she had almost no direct experience with slavery, she was enormously sympathetic to the plight of slaves in the United States. When one of Stowe's two young children died, she would write: "It was at his dying bed and at his grave that I learned what a poor slave mother may feel when her child is torn away from her."[100]

The book was *Uncle Tom's Cabin, or Life Among the Lowly,* a novel that focused on the cruelty of those who own slaves and, with great sympathy, on the victims of slavery. Uncle Tom was a kind, elderly slave who is killed before the

The daughter of Lyman Beecher, a prominent New England Congregationalist minister, Harriet Beecher Stowe lived in Cincinnati, Ohio, for 18 years. It was there where she first encountered fugitive slaves who escaped across the Ohio River to freedom. Stowe is pictured here with her father (center) and brother Henry Ward, in 1860.

novel's end, beaten to death by his owner. Stowe wrote her book to present a sympathetic picture of American slaves. Before she penned her influential work, Stowe had only spent a week in the South. The visit, however, had changed her. As she later wrote to a friend, "I have often felt that much that is in that book had its root in the awful scenes and bitter sorrow of that summer."[101] Her sister-in-law had been pressing Stowe to write something popular on behalf of the abolitionist cause, which she had postponed for a year or two because she had a baby at home who occupied a great deal of time. She finally did put pen to paper in the early 1850s, after the enactment of the Fugitive Slave Act of 1850. She began to write one Sunday afternoon after her return from church, where, she later claimed, "the tragic death of the noble Uncle Tom, came to her . . . in a vision."[102]

Stowe's work was first published in 40 serial issues of the abolitionist weekly newspaper the *National Era*, beginning in June 1851. In March 1852, it was published as a two-volume book by John Punchard Jewett. It sold 300,000 copies in the United States within its first year of publication and 1.5 million copies around the world, primarily in Europe. (Many of those copies were printed illegally, pirated by unscrupulous publishers.) Its popularity was unprecedented. No work of fiction had ever sold that many copies. It was popular among all classes of readers. Queen Victoria cried as she read it, as did the wife of the British novelist and political reformer Charles Dickens. How many American readers, on the basis of that book, changed their minds and opposed the institution of slavery will never be known. The impact of the novel, however, spread across the nation in great ripples.

CALL FOR POPULAR SOVEREIGNTY

The next great controversies over slavery that affected the abolitionist cause unfolded after 1854. That year, new leadership was redirecting the U.S. Senate. The old-line leaders of the previous generation—John C. Calhoun, Henry Clay, and Daniel Webster—had died a few years earlier. The next generation included such men as Stephen Douglas of Illinois, a "short, shrewd, and ambitious"[103] politician who put legislation before his colleagues in regard to the organization of a territory from the old Louisiana Territory. After his bill was changed to create two territories instead of one, it called for the organization of a western territory, Kansas. The true motivation for Douglas's bill, which became the Kansas-Nebraska Act, was to clear the way for the construction of the first rail line to cross the United States from the Atlantic to the Pacific. Douglas, from Illinois, was determined for the line to pass through the northern part of the country so that the eastern terminus of the line would be established in the northern Illinois city of Chicago. (Douglas did own slaves himself, 140 in all, but he claimed they had nothing to do with his decision to support the expansion of slavery into new parts of the West.)

The real controversy of Douglas's new legislation, however, was to create the potential for slavery to enter the northern half of the former Louisiana Territory, even though the Missouri Compromise of more than 30 years earlier had prohibited slavery there. Douglas's logic was, to some, irrefutable: "If the people of Kansas want a slaveholding state, let them have it, and if they want a free state they have a right to it, and it is not for the people of Illinois, or Missouri, or New York, or Kentucky, to complain, whatever the decision of the people of Kansas may be."[104]

At the center of Douglas's legislation was a new political concept: popular sovereignty. It would be up to the voters to decide for or against slavery in a given territory. The decision would not remain in the hands of the federal government or of the states, but with the people of the territories. As for the abolitionist movement, the Kansas-Nebraska Act was met with opposition at all fronts. That summer, during a Fourth of July rally, William Lloyd Garrison would burn a copy of the U.S. Constitution and declare it a covenant with hell.

BLEEDING KANSAS

With Kansas and Nebraska now open to slavery, the region of the West exploded in violence. Even in Douglas's home

(continues on page 96)

THE FUGITIVE SLAVE ACT OF 1850 AND THE BURNS CASE

As the new decade of the 1850s opened, the U.S. Congress once again felt compelled to put together a political compromise to stave off the possible dissolution of the Union. Under the Compromise of 1850, which established California as a free state, the new, tough Fugitive Slave Act of 1850 became reality. This law required Northern law officials to aid in the recapture of escaped slaves in the Northern states. The law greatly angered not only abolitionists but also significant numbers of Americans who were otherwise uncommitted on the slavery issue. Abolitionist newspapers began to print stories of blacks who had found freedom in the North and who, under the new law, were returned to a life of slavery. One of the most notorious and emotional cases took place in Boston four years after the Fugitive Slave Act of 1850 was created.

The subject of the case was a black slave named Anthony Burns. In 1854, Burns was 24 years old, an intelligent young slave who had taught himself to read and write. He had been held in Virginia and "treated well by his master."* Burns's master trusted him and had allowed him a significant amount of freedom to travel throughout the commonwealth. That freedom had given Burns the opportunity, in February 1854, to escape to Boston as a stowaway in a boat.

Once he found his way to Boston, Burns took a job in a clothing store. He made a mistake when he sent a letter to his brother, who was still held as a slave in the South. The letter was intercepted by Burns's owner, and the hunt for Burns was on. A warrant was issued by a judge in Suffolk County, Virginia, for the arrest of Burns. By May, "under circumstances that indicated careful planning,"** authorities were compelled to arrest Burns, then place him in custody in the federal courthouse in Boston. Abolitionists throughout the city rushed into action. Thousands gathered in the city's Faneuil Hall to protest and hear such abolitionist leaders as

Wendell Phillips and Theodore Parker "all but urge violence to prevent the rendition of Anthony Burns."*** A mob of black and white abolitionists marched on the courthouse where Burns was being held. They smashed the building's windows and broke open the front entrance. Authorities

A fugitive slave from Virginia, Anthony Burns was captured by slave hunters in Boston in 1854. Despite protests from many Bostonians, Burns was returned to his owner, Charles F. Suttle, who brought him back to Virginia. The scenes of Burns's life are depicted in this circa 1855 engraving.

attempted to stop them in the courthouse lobby, leading to a fight that resulted in the death of a volunteer deputy. Only when a unit of marines from neighboring Charlestown and

(continues)

(continued)

an artillery company were called in were the rioters driven from the building. Despite the protests, the decision to send Burns back to Virginia and slavery remained firm.

On the day Burns was taken from Boston, perhaps 50,000 citizens of the city and the surrounding towns gathered in the streets in protest. Every soldier in the city was assigned to line the streets on Burns's route from the courthouse to a waiting U.S. revenue cutter in Boston Harbor. Fifteen thousand troops who marched the former slave to his new destiny passed buildings draped in black as a sign of mourning. American flags hung from flagpoles and windows upside down in protest, and "a huge coffin labeled 'Liberty' was suspended across State Street."[†] The protests would not die down. On the Fourth of July, a rally was held in Framingham, Massachusetts, to protest Burns's return to slavery. Speakers included the writer Henry David Thoreau. William Lloyd Garrison was there, as well. He took a copy of the Fugitive Slave Act of 1850, put a flame to it, and, with the gathered crowd, watched as it burned to ash. Then, an angry Garrison spoke: "And let all the people say, Amen."[††] Throughout the assembled throng, the word "Amen" was on everyone's lips. Before he finished his fiery protest that day, Garrison would burn a copy of the U.S. Constitution.

---

[*] Quoted in Louis Filler, *The Crusade Against Slavery, 1830–1860* (New York: Harper & Row, 1960), 214.

[**] Ibid.

[***] Ibid.

[†] James Oliver Horton and Lois E. Horton, *Slavery and the Making of America* (New York: Oxford University Press, 2005), 156.

[††] Filler, 216.

(continued from page 93)

state of Illinois, many opposed the new bill pushed through Congress by their senator. Douglas would claim that "his way home to Illinois that spring was lit by the light of his own burning effigies."[105] Another Illinois political figure was highly critical of the Kansas-Nebraska Act, former congressman and Illinois lawyer Abraham Lincoln. Lincoln stated: "The spirit of Seventy-Six [1776] and the spirit of Nebraska are utter antagonists. Little by little . . . we have been giving up the old for the new faith . . . we began by declaring that all men are created equal, but now from the beginning we have run down to the other declaration, that for some men to enslave others is 'a sacred right of self-government.'"[106]

Throughout the following four or five years, Kansas experienced bloodshed as proslavery supporters raided antislavery communities, and Kansas abolitionists murdered slavery advocates. The territory became known as Bleeding Kansas. One of Lyman Beecher's sons, Henry Ward Beecher, organized a New England Emigration Aid Society and encouraged his fellow New Englanders to move to Kansas. Beecher even suggested that what Kansas abolitionists needed more than anything was guns, so he arranged for the shipment of hundreds of Sharps rifles to the contested territory, weapons that would come to be called "Beecher's Bibles." In the confusion of territorial politics, by 1856, Kansas was struggling with two conflicting territorial governments—proslavery and antislavery.

The trouble in Kansas and the hated Kansas-Nebraska Act also had other political ramifications. Many Northerners blamed both the Democrats and the Whigs, abandoned their parties, and organized support for a new political party—the Republican Party—which was established in Racine, Wisconsin, before the end of the year. The Whig Party soon withered away, and the Democrats split between Northern and Southern wings, never to rejoin. As for Southern Whigs, they typically realigned themselves with the Democrats or a short-lived party known as the Know-Nothings.

8

Hurtling Toward War

In 1856, politics and violence would come together in places other than Kansas. On May 19, just two days before the proslavery raid and sack of Lawrence, Kansas, Charles Sumner, a Massachusetts abolitionist senator, would take the floor during a senate session, and deliver what would be called "The Crime Against Kansas" speech. In it, the abolitionist politician decried the actions of the Border Ruffians, proslavery Missourians who had entered Kansas to intervene with the territory's slave-based politics, as "hirelings picked from the drunken spew and vomit of an uneasy civilization."[107] In his denunciation of the Kansas-Nebraska Act, Sumner was critical of one of his fellow senators, Andrew Pickens Butler from South Carolina. Sumner accused Butler of having "chosen a mistress to whom he has made his vows, and who . . . though polluted in the sight of the world, is chaste in his sight—I mean the harlot slavery."[108] During Sumner's two-day speech, Andrew P. Butler was not present in the Senate chamber.

NEW CLASHES OVER SLAVERY

On May 22, Sumner was attacked by a nephew of Butler's, a member of the House of Representatives named Preston Brooks. Brooks caught Sumner at his desk when the Senate was not in session and beat him with his gold-headed rattan cane. Brooks later described his actions to reporters outside the U.S. Capitol: "I gave him about thirty first rate stripes. . . . Towards the last, he bellowed like a calf. I wore my cane out completely but saved the head—which is gold."[109] The savage beating would render Sumner unconscious and nearly kill him; his recovery would take a full three years. After the attack, admirers of Brooks's actions sent him replacement canes. Citizens of Charleston, South Carolina, delivered to Brooks a special cane with an inscription: "Hit him again." Students at the University of Virginia sent Brooks their own collection of fancy canes. News of Brooks's attack on Sumner helped drive John Brown to retaliate by sacking Lawrence. As one of Brown's own sons claimed, the caning of the Massachusetts senator drove his father crazy.

Then, in 1857, one of the worst setbacks for the abolitionist movement took place in the basement chamber of the U.S. Capitol. At that time, justices of the U.S. Supreme Court met in a dark room of the Capitol, where they announced their decision in a case that had been in the American legal system for more than a decade. Dred Scott, a Missouri-held slave, had sued for the freedom of himself, his wife, and their two daughters on the grounds that his owner, a military doctor, had taken them into the free state of Illinois and the free Wisconsin Territory. Scott's claim was that, when he (and later his family) lived on free soil, they were free. Although Scott had won a lower court decision, the Supreme Court, led by 80-year-old Chief Justice Roger B. Taney, himself a slaveholder, wrote the majority decision that determined that Scott's "claim to freedom was not valid because Congress had no authority to exclude slavery from the territories."[110] Taney went even further, declaring that all blacks in the United States, whether slave or free, were not U.S. citizens and, therefore, had no right to sue under

In 1857, the U.S. Supreme Court ruled in *Dred Scott v. Sandford* that slavery was legal in all territories, thus overturning the 1820 Missouri Compromise. Scott had claimed that, because his master had taken him from the slave state of Missouri to the free state of Illinois and Wisconsin Territory, he should be free. This engraving of Dred Scott, his wife, Harriet, and their children, Eliza and Lizzie, appeared in the June 27, 1857, edition of *Frank Leslie's Illustrated* newspaper.

the U.S. Constitution, as Scott had done. Taney's words were wounding to the abolitionist movement in general and to all African Americans, specifically when he wrote that

Scott "had no rights which the white man was bound to respect."[111]

The chorus of protest against the *Dred Scott v. Sandford* decision was immediate and overwhelming. At a rally in Philadelphia, a black abolitionist, Charles Lenox Remond, spoke to an angry crowd of protestors: "We owe no allegiance to the country which grinds us under its iron heel and treats us like dogs. The time has gone by for colored people to talk of patriotism."[112] Frances Ellen Watkins Harper, another black abolitionist, vented her anger against the Dred Scott decision at a different rally, deriding the U.S. government as "the arch traitor to liberty, as shown by the Fugitive Slave Law and the Dred Scott decision."[113] Only Frederick Douglass saw anything good that might come of the Dred Scott decision. He believed that, because the Supreme Court's position was outrageously incorrect, slavery would become so unpopular with Americans that it would be abolished in short order:

> The Supreme Court . . . [was] not the only power in the world. We, the abolitionists and the colored people, should meet this decision, unlooked for and monstrous as it appears, in a cheerful spirit. The very attempts to blot out forever the hopes of an enslaved people may be one necessary link in the chain of events preparatory to the complete overthrow of the whole slave system.[114]

Across the North, as a sign of protest, African Americans began to form black military associations intended to provide protection for America's now disenfranchised black population.

EXPANDING CRISIS

A new level of crisis was overtaking the country. Perhaps never before in the history of the United States were emotions running so high over the issue of slavery, its expansion westward, and whether the South's power would, in short order, take complete control of the country. In the meantime, a new president had been elected in 1856: James Buchanan, a Democrat from Pennsylvania. Buchanan, though, never had a handle on the events that were unfolding with great speed and high emotion. In fact, President Buchanan did almost nothing to address the slavery issue in the late 1850s. He played no role, even as the country spiraled out of control, ever closer to disunion, secession, and, perhaps, civil war. Meanwhile, William Lloyd Garrison and several of his followers spoke publicly in favor of disunion of the United States as the only means to end the long national nightmare of slavery and slaveholding.

The position was just another form of extremism for the abolitionists, but everything indicated that Southerners would stop at nothing to preserve slavery in American life. Everything seemed to be going the way of the proslavery Southerners:

> [By] the later 1850s, the South seemed stronger than ever. Its economic power had become so great that it could not be ignored. Cotton had become America's most valuable export, more valuable, in fact, than everything else the nation exported to the world combined. The worth of slaves increased correspondingly, so that on the eve of the Civil War it was greater than the total dollar value of all the nation's banks, railroads, and manufacturing. The South was able to translate its economic power into political power. By 1860, slaveholders and their sympathizers controlled the Supreme Court and the major committees of Congress and had a strong support in the president, Pennsylvania-born James Buchanan.[115]

The failure of John Brown's October 1859 raid on Harpers Ferry and his attempt to foment a slave rebellion that might sweep the nation continued the status quo:

Southerners generally vilified Brown, whereas Northerners were split, thinking Brown either a hero, or a villain.

FAILURES OF ABOLITIONISM

For decades, the abolitionists had fought the good fight to make their fellow Americans understand the evils of slavery and the wrongness of slaveholding. Some of the movement's leaders— William Lloyd Garrison, Harriet Tubman, Wendell Phillips, and Frederick Douglass—had, by 1860, spent the majority of their adult years campaigning, preaching, lecturing, marching, rallying, and pleading to Americans that the institution of slavery was wrong, and that the United States was a land where liberty and democracy could not go hand in hand with slavery and racism. Slavery continued to exist, however, with the arrival of yet another decade of the nineteenth century. Had the efforts of so many of slavery's lifelong opponents been for nothing? Was slavery destined not only to survive but also to thrive and spread into every western territory and, indeed, even into the free states themselves?

Throughout much of the half century prior to 1860, the free North and the slaveholding South had drifted increasingly apart. Slavery had long divided Americans before the secession of many of the slaveholding states from the Union from December 1860 through the first six months of 1861. The abolitionist voice had not gone unheard, however. Many Southerners opposed slavery during the 1800s. Many were up-country, poor farmers who did not own a single slave and who often despised the prosperous planters whose grand estates relied on slave labor. Certainly, significant numbers of Northerners also had come to dislike slavery. From the 1830s, the voices of Garrison, Douglass, and many others had not fallen on deaf ears. Their words, as well as significant political events, such as the passage of the Fugitive Slave Act of 1850, the publication of Stowe's emotional and sympathetic novel, the Kansas-Nebraska Act, popular sovereignty, and the Dred Scott decision, had all managed to build additional support for those individuals who opposed slavery. The South may have managed great gains in the cause to retain slavery and spread it to the territories, but opponents of slavery were not in the least prepared to surrender their cause.

The year 1860 would prove to be the turning point in the campaign against slavery. In that year's presidential election, the Republican Party selected Illinois lawyer Abraham Lincoln as its candidate. The party members chose Lincoln because they thought him a moderate in his antislavery views. He was a compromise candidate, "everyone's second choice in a convention dominated by more celebrated politicians."[116] Lincoln had spoken publicly for years against the spread of slavery into the western territories. He did not believe, however, that a U.S. president had the power to outlaw slavery where it already existed. On this topic, he told his supporters: "Hold firm, as with a chain of steel. The tug has to come, and better now than any time hereafter."[117]

Two years earlier, Lincoln had challenged fellow Illinoisan Stephen Douglas for his Senate seat and lost. The two men had campaigned hard and had engaged in a series of seven debates that had proven lively and popular with the state's voters. Douglas had defeated Lincoln, but not through the polls. At that time, senators were selected by their state legislators, not by the direct vote of the people. The campaign, however, had given Lincoln a clear taste for power politics, and he became known throughout the country. His name had, during the intervening two years, become a household word. In the 1860 presidential election, he would face Stephen Douglas a second time. Douglas was selected as the Democratic Party's nominee. When he was chosen in the summer of 1860 at the party's convention in

Slavery was the primary issue in the 1860 presidential election. The Southern states supported former vice president and Southern Democrat John C. Breckinridge (center) from Kentucky, while the Northern states largely supported the Republican candidate, Abraham Lincoln (left). The Northern Democratic candidate, Stephen Douglas (right), is also pictured here.

Charleston, South Carolina, the delegates from the Deep South states had walked out in protest. Douglas had lost their support during the struggle over the Kansas-Nebraska Act, Bleeding Kansas, and other positions that he had taken on slavery's expansion that Southerners did not like. These Southerners soon organized the Southern Democratic Party, holding their own convention in Baltimore. They nominated Vice President John C. Breckinridge of Kentucky as their candidate. Still other Southerners, those opposed to the ever-increasing talk of separation from the United States, made up yet a fourth party, the Constitutional Union Party, and selected John Bell from Tennessee as their candidate.

LINCOLN AND SLAVERY

When 51-year-old Abraham Lincoln accepted the Republican Party's nomination for president in 1860, the future of the United States and the existence of slavery were set to change. His opponent, Stephen Douglas, would carry the Democratic Party's standard as their candidate, even as Southern Democrats split off and formed parties of their own. These two Illinois men, then, held the future of the United States in their hands in 1860. Who were these men, and what were their positions on slavery?

Abraham Lincoln was born and raised a westerner. His birth state was Kentucky, and he grew up in Indiana and Illinois. One reason his father had moved the family when Lincoln was only a youth was "partly on account of slavery."* As a Baptist, Thomas Lincoln, Abraham's father, considered slavery a sin, along with "profanity, intoxication, horse racing, and other human vices."** When Lincoln was 19 years old, he and a cousin named Dennis Hanks had taken a trip down the Mississippi River to New Orleans. There he had witnessed the sale of a young black woman on the slave market. The scene had sickened Lincoln. Afterward, he had told his cousin: "By God, boys, if I ever get a chance to hit [slavery], I'll hit it and hit it hard."*** When he served a single term in the House of Representatives during the 1840s, Lincoln had spoken out against the wrongs of slavery and, in 1849, had introduced a bill in the House that abolished slavery in the nation's capital. The following decade, in a speech in Peoria, Illinois, Lincoln had referred to the Declaration of Independence and had spoken of slavery as "a total violation of this principle."† Despite these public and private positions on slavery,

When the election was held in November, Lincoln emerged the victor, as his three opponents only managed to split the Democratic Party's vote. Lincoln would be the next president. The reality of it had barely sunk in when South Carolina held a state convention and voted in December to secede from the Union. Six other Southern states followed in rapid succession. Within six months of the 1860 election,

Lincoln was not prepared to deny slavery to Southerners where it already existed. Thus, he was not an abolitionist, but one who wanted to contain the institution.

Before Lincoln and Douglas faced each other in the 1860 presidential campaign, they had competed for the same Illinois seat in the U.S. Senate two years earlier. That senatorial campaign served as a dress rehearsal for both men and their later bids for the White House. It had also made fairly clear their differing opinions on slavery and its expansion into the western territories. The two candidates battled each other in seven statewide debates held from August to early October, one in each of the state's seven congressional districts. Slavery remained at the center of these debates.

As one of the authors of popular sovereignty, Douglas argued that the expansion of slavery should rest in the hands of the people in the territories directly affected. He stated that "the signers of the *Declaration* [*of Independence*] had no reference to the Negro whatever, when they declared all men to be created equal."[††] As Lincoln countered Douglas's arguments, he did not state that he believed in the social or political equality of America's blacks. He did, though, confirm his view on other issues: "I believe that the right of property in a slave is not distinctly and expressly affirmed in the Constitution."[†††]

---

[*] James Oliver Horton and Lois E. Horton, *Slavery and the Making of America* (New York: Oxford University Press, 2005), 167.

[**] Ibid.

[***] Ibid.

[†] Ibid.

[††] David Herbert Donald, *Lincoln* (New York: Simon and Schuster, 1995), 220.

[†††] Horton, 168.

these states would create their own nation, the Confederate States of America. By mid-April 1861, following an attack on the Union-held Fort Sumter in Charleston, South Carolina, the war began. With this single and bloodless attack (no one was killed during the shelling), both North and South were plunged into war.

9

Successful Campaign

Although issues revolving around slavery and its advance into the western territories were crucial causes of the American Civil War in 1861, the war did not begin directly because of slavery. With Lincoln's election, the South believed its way of life, which included slavery, would be threatened. Secession became the answer. The war opened when Lincoln refused to surrender control of Fort Sumter, the federal military installation in Charleston. At the start of the war, the focus was on the South's withdrawal from the Union and the North's resolve to force the Confederate states back into the United States. "Preservation of the Union" was the rallying cry of the North.

ABOLITIONISM AND THE WAR

Slavery and its role in the war could not be ignored. Black abolitionist Frederick Douglass understood that the war would, in time, place the issue of slavery and the question of its future existence at the forefront: "The American people . . . may refuse to recognize it for a time," he wrote, "but the 'inexorable logic of events' will force it upon them in the end; that the war now being waged in this land is a war for and against slavery."[118] Perhaps few understood at the time just how right Douglass was.

As for William Lloyd Garrison, "he welcomed the war as the only means of freeing the slave."[119] Once the war began in the spring of 1861, Garrison's abolitionist philosophy and his view of the U.S. government and the U.S. Constitution underwent a fundamental change. Although earlier, Garrison had decried the government and lambasted the Constitution as a covenant with hell, the war caused him to change his mind. He made clear this change in his philosophy in a three-column editorial in the October 4, 1861, edition of *The Liberator*. He reminded abolitionists that he and they had campaigned for a decade under the watch phrase "No Union with slaveholders."[120] He stated that the slogan had been meant to gain the attention of the American people. It had never meant that abolitionists were disloyal to the government, nor were they going to be disloyal now that the federal government of the North had gone to war with the Confederate South. Garrison, who had condemned the Constitution previously, now praised it as a document that guaranteed basic freedoms, such as the right of free speech and free press, "and these rights were all that the Garrisonians had ever claimed."[121] Garrison, it appeared, was on board with the government and its military struggle against the Confederacy. In 1861, as federal troops marched into the South, the lifelong abolitionist from Boston "hailed it as God's machine for dispensing retribution."[122]

Even with support from abolitionists such as Garrison for the military effort against the South, the antislavery agitators had their doubts about Lincoln and his commitment to end slavery. When Lincoln spoke to Congress in December 1861, he did not even mention emancipation. "What a wishy-washy message from the President!"[123] Garrison wrote.

ORDERS AGAINST SLAVERY

The joint view of Douglass and Garrison, that the war was about slavery and its demise, may well have first manifested itself on the battlefield. Federal troops advanced onto Southern soil in an effort to bring about the South's defeat. As Union troops captured plantations and Southern communities, commanders sometimes took the opportunity to liberate slaves held locally, even though they had no express order from Lincoln, their commander in chief, to do so.

On two occasions, Lincoln's own commanders moved faster and more decisively against slavery than did the president. Within months of the opening of the war, in August 1861, General John C. Fremont, the Republican candidate for president in 1856, declared martial law in Missouri and announced that all slaves held by those who supported the Confederacy were freed. The news of Fremont's unilateral move had a ripple effect across the country. Those slaveholders who had remained loyal to the federal government and not participated in secession were outraged. Others, especially the abolitionists, were ecstatic. Garrison praised Fremont's "wise, beneficent and masterly procedure."[124] When abolitionist leader Wendell Phillips praised Fremont during a lecture, the audience took up a thunderous applause "once he mentioned the magic name of Fremont."[125] When Lincoln received news of Fremont's actions, however, the president was furious. After Fremont refused to amend his order, President Lincoln did it for him; he later removed Fremont from his command and replaced him with General David Hunter.

Nine months later, that same Union commander, who had been transferred to the Department of the South (a federal military department assigned to South Carolina, Georgia, and Florida), made his own move against slavery. In May

1862, General Hunter announced that slavery was abolished within the territory of his department. Whereas Fremont's decision had an impact on slaveholders in a crucial border state, Hunter's decision affected only "rebellious owners in the Confederacy itself."[126] Again, an angry and frustrated Lincoln canceled Hunter's abolition announcement.

In the meantime, members of the U.S. Congress took more decisive action. In July 1861, with the war only a few months old, legislators passed a resolution declaring that it was "no part of the duty of the soldiers of the United States to capture and return fugitive slaves."[127] The following month, Congress passed an act that allowed for the confiscation of slaves whose owners had permitted them to be used in support of the Confederacy. In time, all slaves held in Confederate states came to be considered vital to the Confederate cause, which made them "contraband of war" and allowed federal troops to remove them from Southern ownership. Slaves who knew of the act of Congress escaped from their masters and sought refuge behind federal lines. Six months later, in March 1862, Congress took another step in its efforts to abolish slavery. A new law prohibited any Union military personnel from returning escaped slaves to their "rightful" masters. On the heels of this move, Congress abolished slavery in the District of Columbia. By June, Congress banned slavery in all western territories, "settling the issue that for so long had disturbed the public peace."[128] New Yorker George Templeton Strong would write of these moves by Congress: "Only the damndest of 'damned abolitionists' dreamed of such [things] a year ago. John Brown's soul is marching on, with the people after it."[129]

THE EMANCIPATION PROCLAMATION

Within a short time, President Lincoln would take significant action himself. Despite his earlier moves against generals

On September 22, 1862, President Abraham Lincoln declared the Emancipation Proclamation, which promised freedom to all slaves living in the Confederate states that did not return to the Union by the end of the year. Lincoln purposely waited to make the announcement until after the Union Army's first major victory in the Civil War, which took place at Antietam Creek in Maryland, five days before the proclamation.

Fremont and Hunter, President Lincoln would not completely stand against the separation of Southern slaveholders from their property. By the summer of 1862, he had made the decision to issue a presidential order to free all slaves being held in the states of the Confederacy, from Virginia to Texas. He knew the value of such a strategic move. Emancipation of the slaves would, Lincoln hoped, destroy the Southern economy by removing an important labor force; in addition, Southerners would lose one of their most important investments—the slaves themselves. Lincoln, though, delayed public announcement of his Emancipation Proclamation until the Union Army won a decisive battle over the Confederacy. Otherwise, his important blow against slavery would have had no real weight, appearing as little more, in the words of Lincoln's secretary of State William Henry Seward, than "the last shriek, on our retreat."[130] That victory came in September, when Union forces defeated Confederate general Robert E. Lee's Army of Northern Virginia in a large-scale battle in Maryland called Antietam (the Southern name is Sharpsburg). On September 22, just five days after the Antietam engagement, Lincoln announced his Emancipation Proclamation. It was a bold move, and Lincoln knew it. It was a move of which he was also proud. "If my name ever goes into history," he claimed, "it was for this act."[131] Members of Lincoln's cabinet were generally supportive of his move. At a dinner party in Washington, D.C., Lincoln's secretary, John Hay, observed how "everyone seemed to feel a new sort of exhilarating life. The President's proclamation had freed them as well as the slaves. They gleefully . . . called each other abolitionists and seemed to enjoy the novel accusation of appropriating that horrible name."[132]

LINCOLN'S UNCONVINCED CRITICS

Abolitionists, although appreciative of Lincoln's proclamation, were not completely satisfied. By this executive order, slavery was not abolished on American soil. The proclamation applied only to slaves held in states and parts of states not yet occupied by federal military forces. Slaves in the border states that had not seceded—Missouri, Maryland, Delaware, and Kentucky—were not included. Wendell Phillips was among the dissatisfied. Lincoln, he said, "is only stopping on the edge of Niagara, to pick up and save a few chips. He and they will go over together."[133] Many Northerners, however, took the president's Emancipation Proclamation seriously. They believed it began the downfall of American slavery.

In contrast to Phillips's broad disappointment and disapproval of Lincoln's actions toward the eradication of slavery during the war, William Lloyd Garrison became, increasingly, an advocate of the president. He gained a new respect for Lincoln as the Union military effort became bogged down through 1862 and into 1863. Garrison told his fellow abolitionists, those who would listen to him, to be patient and "let Northern patriotism do its work."[134] He sent out instructions to his followers to turn down the volume of their agitation and give the president and the war a chance to bring about what the antislavery supporters had been seeking for so long. Sometimes, he was driven to support Lincoln in the face of harsh criticism from Wendell Phillips. Uncharacteristically, Garrison even wrote the following: "I have always believed that the Anti-Slavery cause has aroused against it a great deal of uncalled for hostility in consequence of extravagance of speech and want of tact and good judgment, on the part of some most desirous to promote its advancement."[135] These were strange words coming from the political agitator who had turned his back on the U.S. government, its founding documents, and its democratic ideals.

NEW FREEDOM

Although total emancipation would not take place for a few more years, Lincoln announced that his executive order would take effect on January 1, 1863. Those who had opposed slavery for so long counted down the days to year's end and, on New Year's Eve, counted down the hours and minutes to mark the New Year of freedom. Blacks across the country, as well as many white well-wishers, celebrated the moment and gathered in public places and in churches, where steeple bells tolled the end of slavery in the yet to be defeated South. When word reached the city of Boston, the long-standing center of abolitionism, a large crowd began to gather in the city's music hall to watch the clock move to midnight. Present on the hall's stage were some of the greatest leaders of the abolitionist movement, including William Lloyd Garrison, Harriet Beecher Stowe, and Frederick Douglass. Stowe was received by a tumult of applause as "she rose from her seat in the balcony, grateful tears in her eyes."[136] Douglass described what he witnessed that evening:

> The effect of this announcement was startling beyond description, and the scene was wild and grand. Joy and gladness exhausted all forms of expression, from shouts of praise to sobs and tears . . . a Negro preacher [Reverend Charles Bennet Ray] a man of wonderful vocal power, expressed the heartfelt emotion of the hour, when he led all voices in the anthem, "Sound the loud timbrel o'er Egypt's dark sea, Jehovah hath triumphed, his people were free."[137]

Throughout the music hall, Douglass wrote later, "Men, women, young and old, were up; hats and bonnets were in the air . . . . There was shouting and singing, 'Glory Hallelujah,' 'Old John Brown,' 'Marching On,' and 'Blow Ye, the Trumpet Blow!'—till we got up such a state of enthusiasm that almost anything seemed witty—and entirely appropriate to the glorious occasion."[138]

Just days after Lincoln's announcement of the Emancipation Proclamation, Garrison spoke to the Massachusetts Anti-Slavery Society: "Thirty years ago, it was midnight with the anti-slavery cause; now it is the bright noon of day with the sun shining in his meridian splendor."[139] Beginning January 1, 1863, William Lloyd Garrison became a "tenacious Unionist" who would strongly defend President Abraham Lincoln.[140] In 1864, when Lincoln ran for reelection as president, Garrison would write editorials in *The Liberator* in support of Lincoln.

Throughout the South, groups of black slaves were gathered together by federal troops as the Emancipation Proclamation was read aloud to them. In a contraband camp outside Washington, D.C., a former slave recalled how a daughter had been sold away from him. "Now no more of that,"[141] he said. In South Carolina, a newly raised black regiment under the command of a Boston abolitionist named Thomas Wentworth Higginson heard the words of the proclamation read by the unit's chaplain and, in celebration, erupted into endless shouting. Then Higginson unfurled a new American flag as his men began to sing "My Country 'Tis of Thee, Sweet Land of Liberty, of Thee I Sing."[142] The Emancipation Proclamation was an immense obstacle for the future of slavery in the United States. With the sheer weight and force of the office of the president of the United States and of the federal government behind the emancipation, "the institution of slavery cracked, crumbled, and collapsed after January 1, 1863."[143] Through the decades after that momentous night, and well into the twentieth century, New Year's Day would be celebrated in black communities as Emancipation Day.

Lincoln's decision to liberate the slaves on Confederate soil represented one of the most important public policy shifts for the president during the war. With the proclamation, another change soon took place. Blacks were allowed to enlist in the Union Army, with Lincoln pledging they would be "received into the armed service of the United States to

After the Emancipation Proclamation, slaves were permitted to serve in the Union Army. By the end of the war, approximately 180,000 blacks had served in the Union Army in more than 160 "colored" regiments, including the 54th Massachusetts. Pictured here are two unidentified black soldiers who served in the Union Army during the war.

garrison forts, positions, stations, and other places, and to man vessels of all sorts in said service."[144] Blacks would now be fighting on behalf of both the Union and against slavery. Before the end of the war, nearly 180,000 black Americans served in the Union Army in all-black units (although they were commanded by white officers). Of that number, 37,000 would die fighting for their country and for the freedom of other blacks. Among those who fought were two sons of Frederick Douglass, Lewis and Charles. They both joined one of two regiments of black troops their father helped organize, the Massachusetts 54th. William Lloyd Garrison's son George also joined the 54th, as a second lieutenant, despite his father's wishes. William Lloyd Garrison was, personally, a pacifist. When the 54th engaged in its most famous fight, a direct frontal assault on Fort Wagner outside Charleston, South Carolina, Harriet Tubman was with them and served the troops their last meal before the assault. She also tended their wounds after the assault failed and even helped bury some of the dead black soldiers.

THE PROCLAMATION'S SHORTCOMINGS

Even as the Emancipation Proclamation went into effect on the first day of 1863, the nation's abolitionists were not satisfied. The proclamation had provided only half a loaf. The document did not cover all slaves in all places in the United States. Later that same month, a delegation of Boston abolitionists visited the White House and expressed their concerns to President Lincoln. Among them was Wendell Phillips. Phillips asked the president whether he thought the Emancipation Proclamation was working. Lincoln was positive, believing the country was not dissatisfied with anything "except our lack of military success."[145] When some abolitionists questioned whether Lincoln was pushing against slavery hard enough, the president answered that "he did not believe his administration would have been supported by the country in a policy of emancipation at an earlier stage of the war."[146]

Although the meeting between the abolitionists and President Lincoln went well and remained cordial, some antislavery advocates, especially Phillips, would remain constant thorns in the side of the president. They wanted the ongoing war between the North and South to lead to the destruction of slavery. Lincoln remained aloof on the subject and insisted that his most important goal of the war was to put the Union back together. If doing so meant slavery must be kept, he was noted as saying, then he would follow that course. Phillips would soon launch a campaign that called for a constitutional amendment to end slavery. A year to the day following the public enactment of the Emancipation Proclamation, Phillips would write in the year's first issue of *The Liberator*: "What I ask of Mr. Lincoln in his behalf is, an amendment of the Constitution which his advice to Congress would pass in sixty days, that hereafter there shall be neither slavery nor involuntary servitude in any State of this Union."[147]

THE THIRTEENTH AMENDMENT

Such an amendment would move toward becoming a reality throughout 1864. In January 1865, by a vote of 121 to 24, the U.S. Congress passed the Thirteenth Amendment to the U.S. Constitution, which provided for the complete abolition of slavery in the United States. Nearly a year would pass, however, before the amendment was ratified by the states in December. With the passage of the Thirteenth Amendment, America was changed forever. To those who understood its importance, the day represented a watershed of political redirection, social and racial alteration, and a fundamental difference for the country and its future: Never again would one American hold another American in bondage. Freedom had become a national birthright, and Congress had established itself as its guardian.

The end of the war would soon follow. General William Tecumseh Sherman had already reached Atlanta and marched his way across Georgia and the Carolinas, crushing the capacity of those states to wage war any longer. Within months of the passage of the Thirteenth Amendment, the Confederate capital, Richmond, Virginia, would be in Union hands, and General Lee would soon find himself surrounded by General Ulysses S. Grant's federal forces, with no place left to fight. On April 9, 1865, the bloodiest war in American history would finally end in southwestern Virginia at a crossroads community called Appomattox Court House. It was there that Lee surrendered his army to Grant and the war came to an end. The South had been defeated, and slavery was no more.

Five days later, on April 14, four years to the day since the surrender of Fort Sumter in Charleston Harbor had opened the war, a noontime ceremony was held at the ruined fort. Present at the symbolic event was the fort's former Union commander, Major General Robert Anderson, who had surrendered his post in 1861. Also present were several abolitionists, including Henry Ward Beecher and William Lloyd Garrison, who had been invited to the event. Also in attendance at the ceremony were 4,000 former slaves.

The day was "clear and beautiful."[148] Cannons boomed from the forts that lined the Charleston coast. The artillery in Fort Sumter was fired for the first time since it was silenced in defeat four years earlier. Out in Charleston Harbor, ships "were dressed up with flaunting flags."[149] Everywhere within sight of Fort Sumter, U.S. flags flew in the nearly cloudless sky; everywhere, except Fort Sumter. Then, General Anderson stepped forward near the flagpole towering above the fort and raised a tattered American flag over the fort, the same one he had taken down when he surrendered in the spring of 1861. At first, the flag "hung limp . . . a weather-beaten, frayed and shell-torn old flag," as a Northern woman described it. "But when it had crept clear of the shelter of the walls, a sudden breath of wind caught it and it shook its folds and flew straight above us."[150]

Henry Ward Beecher had been asked to deliver the principal address and so spoke that day. Garrison, too, gave a brief oration, in which he spoke as directly as ever about the cause to which he had dedicated his life: "I hate slavery as I hate nothing else in the world. It is not only a crime, but the sum of all criminality."[151] The triumph of the moment was multilayered. Fort Sumter had been rededicated, the war was over, and slavery was dead. The abolitionists, along with the nation, had persevered.

The next morning, on April 15, William Lloyd Garrison visited a local Charleston cemetery, located adjacent to St. Phillip's Church. He searched the rows of stones and monuments until he reached one built of brick, topped with a massive slab of marble. Inscribed on the stone was a single name: Calhoun. Garrison stepped forward and placed his hand on the cool marble. Then, he spoke to the dead and addressed America's future: "Down into a deeper grave than this slavery has gone, and for it there is no resurrection."[152]

Eight months later, the Thirteenth Amendment was ratified, and the law went into effect on December 29, 1865. That evening, as the clock neared midnight, William Lloyd Garrison sat at his desk and wrote out his final words for the pages of *The Liberator*. Slavery was dead in the United States and so was the purpose for which his long-standing abolitionist paper had existed. For 35 years, his voice had been constant and clear against the institution he hated more than any other. He was still writing up to the last minute before the paper was set to go to press. When he wrote his last sentence, he placed his pen on his desk, rose from his chair, and went to the composing bench, where he himself set by hand the moveable type for the last paragraph of his last editorial. When he finished, he spoke a friendly goodnight to his printers and went home.

CHRONOLOGY

1500–1850   During these centuries, 10 million African slaves are imported to the Americas.

1619   Dutch ship transports 20 black Africans to Jamestown, Virginia.

1662   Virginia legislature votes that children of slave mothers will be considered slaves.

1688   Group of Quakers in Germantown, Pennsylvania, begin to preach against slavery.

Timeline

1688
Quakers in Germantown, Pennsylvania, begin to preach against slavery

1815
Union Humane Society founded

1821
Benjamin Lundy begins to publish the *Genius of Universal Emancipation*

1619

1828

1619
Dutch ship transports 20 black Africans to Jamestown

1775
Society for the Relief of Free Negroes Unlawfully Held in Bondage founded

1816
American Colonization Society formed

1828
First station of Underground Railroad established

1700   Number of slaves in British colonies of North America constitutes approximately 11 percent of total colonial population.

1729   Antislavery pamphlet is published by Quaker Ralph Sandiford.

1739   Stono Rebellion by slaves in South Carolina leads to killing of 30 whites.

1750   Black slaves constitute 40 percent of the South's population.

1775   Society for the Relief of Free Negroes Unlawfully Held in Bondage is founded in Philadelphia.

1777–1784   During and just after Revolutionary War, Vermont, Massachusetts, New Hampshire,

1831
William Lloyd Garrison begins publication of *The Liberator*

1845
Frederick Douglass publishes his autobiography

1857
Dred Scott v. Sandford

1863
Emancipation Proclamation

1831 ———————————————————— **1865**

1833
American Anti-Slavery Society founded

1852
Harriet Beecher Stowe publishes *Uncle Tom's Cabin*

1859
John Brown raids federal arsenal at Harpers Ferry, Virginia

1865
Thirteenth Amendment ratified

	Pennsylvania, Connecticut, and Rhode Island all abolish slavery within their borders.
1787	Congress of the Confederation adopts Northwest Ordinance, which bans slavery from region.
1792–1793	Eli Whitney invents the cotton gin, making cotton production in the South profitable, which encourages the expansion of slavery.
1815	Benjamin Lundy founds Union Humane Society in Ohio.
1816	American Colonization Society is formed; its goal is to help blacks return to Africa from the United States.
1819	Missouri Territory applies for statehood as slave state.
1820–1821	Congress hammers out Missouri Compromise, which bans slavery from northern portions of original Louisiana Purchase.
1821	Benjamin Lundy begins to publish antislavery paper, the *Genius of Universal Emancipation.*
1828	Reverend John Rankin purchases farm outside Ripley, Ohio, and establishes first station of Underground Railroad; that same year, Benjamin Lundy meets William Lloyd Garrison.
1831	William Lloyd Garrison begins publication of *The Liberator;* later that same year, Nat Turner, a Virginia slave, leads one of bloodiest slave uprisings in American history.
1833	American Anti-Slavery Society is founded in Philadelphia.

1837 Grimké sisters take up cause of abolition and engage in speaking tour in New England.

1838 Garrison and others establish New England Non-Resistant Society; that same year, young Frederick Douglass escapes from slavery.

1840 Abolitionists and others form the Liberty Party, a political party opposed to expansion of slavery into western territories.

1845 Frederick Douglass publishes his autobiography.

1847 Douglass begins to publish his own antislavery paper, *North Star*.

1849 Harriet Tubman escapes from slavery and soon begins to help other slaves escape.

1850 Compromise of 1850 brings California into the Union as a free state even as it creates a stronger, tighter fugitive slave law.

1852 Harriet Beecher Stowe publishes *Uncle Tom's Cabin*.

1854 Fugitive slave Anthony Burns is taken from Boston by government officials and returned to slavery under new Fugitive Slave Law of 1850; that same year, Senator Stephen Douglas introduces popular sovereignty and leads campaign to pass Kansas-Nebraska Act.

1856 John Brown and some followers raid homes of proslavery settlement near Pottawatomie Creek, Kansas, and kill five proslavery settlers; on May 22, Congressman Preston Brooks severely beats Senator Charles Sumner.

1857 U.S. Supreme Court decides *Dred Scott v. Sandford*, declaring Congress has no power to limit slavery in American territory.

1858	Abraham Lincoln and Stephen Douglas engage in series of debates on subject of slavery and its expansion.
1859	On October 16–18, abolitionist John Brown and small band of followers raid federal arsenal at Harpers Ferry, Virginia, intending to launch widespread slave rebellion; raid fails and Brown is arrested; on December 2, Brown is hanged after conviction by a jury of treason against the Commonwealth of Virginia.
1860	Approximately 10,000 American blacks have migrated to Africa to colonize, all since 1816; that same year, Abraham Lincoln is elected president of the United States.
1860–1861	Eleven Southern states secede from the Union and form the Confederate States of America; the Civil War begins in April.
1863	Emancipation Proclamation goes into effect on January 1.
1865	In January, U.S. Congress passes Thirteenth Amendment, which abolishes slavery in United States; in December, Thirteenth Amendment is ratified and becomes part of U.S. Constitution.

NOTES

CHAPTER 1

1. James Oliver Horton and Lois E. Horton, *Slavery and the Making of America* (New York: Oxford University Press, 2005), 161.
2. Quoted in "John Brown." Civil War Home. Available online at *http://www.civilwarhome.com/johnbrownbio.htm*.
3. Ibid.
4. Geoffrey C. Ward, *The Civil War: An Illustrated History* (New York: Alfred A. Knopf, 1990), 2.
5. Louis Ruchames, ed., *John Brown: The Making of a Revolutionary* (New York: Grosset & Dunlap, 1969), 186.
6. Ibid., 188.
7. James McPherson, *Battle Cry of Freedom* (New York: Oxford University Press, 1988), 152.
8. Ibid.
9. Ibid.
10. Ibid., 153.
11. Horton, 161.
12. Ibid.
13. Quoted in "John Brown." Civil War Home. Available online at *http://www.civilwarhome.com/johnbrownbio.htm*.
14. Ibid.
15. Ibid.
16. Ibid.

CHAPTER 2

17. Tim McNeese, *The American Colonies* (St. Louis: Milliken, 2002), 46.
18. Winthrop D. Jordan, "Unthinking Decision: Enslavement of Negroes in America to 1700," in *Interpreting Colonial America: Selected Readings*, James Kirby Martin, ed. (New York: Dodd, Mead & Company, 1974), 167.
19. McNeese, *The American Colonies*, 52.
20. Darlene Clark Hine, *The African-American Odyssey* (Upper Saddle River, N.J.: Prentice Hall, 2005), 68.
21. Ibid.
22. Ibid.
23. Daniel Littlefield, *Revolutionary Citizens: African Americans, 1776–1804* (New York: Oxford University Press, 1997), 21.
24. Louis Filler, *The Crusade Against Slavery, 1830–1860* (New York: Harper & Row, 1960), 13.
25. Tim McNeese, *The Rise and Fall of American Slavery: Freedom Denied, Freedom Gained* (Berkeley Heights,

N.J.: Enslow Publishers, 2004), 55.

CHAPTER 3

26. Lisa W. Strick, "The Black Presence in the Revolution, 1770–1800," in *Freedom to Freedom*, Mildred Bain and Ervin Lewis, eds. (Milwaukee: Purnell Reference Books, 1977), 213.
27. Hine, 78.
28. David Brion Davis, *The Problem of Slavery in the Age of the Revolution, 1770–1823* (Ithaca, N.Y.: Cornell University Press, 1975), 283.
29. Hine, 99.
30. Constance Green, *Eli Whitney and the Birth of American Technology* (New York: HarperCollins, 1956), 45.
31. Ibid., 46.
32. Ward, 12.
33. Ibid.
34. Filler, 15.
35. Ronald G. Walters, *American Reformers, 1815–1860* (New York: Hill and Wang, 1978), 78.
36. Ibid.
37. Ibid.

CHAPTER 4

38. David Goldfield, *The American Journey: A History of the United States* (Upper Saddle River, N.J.: Pearson Education, 2007), 269.
39. Ibid.

40. Horton, 104.
41. Ibid.
42. Alice Dana Adams, *The Neglected Period of Anti-Slavery in America, 1808–1831* (Williamstown, Mass.: Corner House, 1973), 17.
43. Ibid., 18.
44. Ibid., 61.
45. R. E. Banta, *The Ohio* (New York: Rinehart, 1949), 473.
46. Walter Havighurst, *River to the West: Three Centuries of the Ohio* (New York: G. P. Putnam's Sons, 1970), 19–20.
47. Ibid., 243.
48. Ibid.
49. Adams, 24.
50. Ibid., 25.
51. Ibid.
52. Ibid.

CHAPTER 5

53. Hine, 180.
54. Ibid.
55. Benjamin Quarles, *Black Abolitionists* (New York: Oxford University Press, 1969), 16.
56. Hine, 171.
57. Ibid., 181.
58. Quarles, 18.
59. Horton, 112.
60. Ibid.
61. Filler, 53.
62. Quarles, 18.
63. Linda Jacobs Altman, *Slavery and Abolition in American History* (Berkeley Heights, N.J.: Enslow Publishers, 1999), 36.

64. Quarles, 19.
65. Russel B. Nye, *William Lloyd Garrison and the Humanitarian Reformers* (Boston: Little, Brown and Company, 1955), 49.
66. Goldfield, 360.
67. Ibid.
68. Ibid., 297.
69. Hine, 197.
70. Goldfield, 297.
71. Ibid.
72. Ibid.
73. Ibid.
74. Ibid., 362.
75. Tim McNeese, *America's Civil War* (St. Louis: Milliken, 2003), 14.

CHAPTER 6

76. Goldfield, 365.
77. Ibid.
78. Ibid.
79. Ward, 16.
80. Frederick Douglass, *Narrative of the Life of Frederick Douglass*, from *Slave Narratives*, in *The Library of America*, William L. Andrews and Henry Louis Gates, Jr., eds. (New York: Literary Classics of the United States, 2000), 276.
81. Ibid., 284.
82. Goldfield, 365.
83. Ibid.
84. Quoted in Horton, 146.
85. Ibid.
86. Quoted in Hine, 200.
87. Wilbur H. Siebert, *The Underground Railroad*, 1898 Reprint (New York: Arno Press, 1968), 56.
88. R. C. Smedley, *History of the Underground Railroad* (Lancaster, Pa.: Office of the Journal, 1883), 249.
89. Catherine Clinton, *Harriet Tubman: The Road to Freedom* (New York: Little, Brown and Company, 2004), 74.
90. Ibid., 83.
91. Horton, 138.

CHAPTER 7

92. Quoted in Ward, 19.
93. Ibid.
94. Ibid.
95. Ibid.
96. Ibid.
97. Ibid.
98. Horton, 155.
99. Goldfield, 404.
100. Ibid., 403.
101. Ibid., 404.
102. Ward, 19.
103. Ibid., 20.
104. Ibid.
105. Ibid., 21.
106. Ibid.

CHAPTER 8

107. Ward, 21.
108. Hine, 219.
109. Ward, 21.
110. Horton, 158.
111. Ibid.
112. Ibid.
113. Hine, 220.
114. Ibid., 221.
115. Horton, 159.

116. Ward, 26.

117. Ibid.

CHAPTER 9

118. Altman, 94.

119. John L. Thomas, *The Liberator: William Lloyd Garrison; A Biography* (Boston: Little, Brown and Company, 1963), 410.

120. Ibid., 412.

121. Ibid.

122. Ibid.

123. Ibid., 414.

124. Ibid.

125. Ward, 180.

126. Ibid.

127. Ibid.

128. Ibid.,150.

129. Ibid.

130. Ibid.

131. Ibid., 166.

132. Ibid., 167.

133. Ibid.

134. Thomas, 416.

135. Ibid.

136. Ward, 177.

137. Hine, 238.

138. Quoted in Altman, 97.

139. Thomas, 420.

140. Ibid.

141. Ward, 177.

142. Ibid.

143. Hine, 240.

144. Altman, 97.

145. Oscar Sherwin, *Prophet of Liberty: The Life and Times of Wendell Phillips* (New York: Bookman Associates, 1958), 475.

146. Ibid., 476.

147. *The Liberator*, XXXIV, 1 (January 1, 1864).

148. Sherwin, 510.

149. Ibid.

150. Ward, 383.

151. Sherwin, 510.

152. Ibid.

BIBLIOGRAPHY

Adams, Alice Dana. *The Neglected Period of Anti-Slavery in America, 1808–1831*. Williamstown, Mass.: Corner House, 1973.

Banta, R. E. *The Ohio*. New York: Rinehart & Company, 1949.

Blockson, Charles. *The Underground Railroad*. New York: Prentice Hall Press, 1987.

Clinton, Catherine. *Harriet Tubman: The Road to Freedom*. New York: Little, Brown and Company, 2004.

Davis, David Brion. *Inhuman Bondage: The Rise and Fall of Slavery in the New World*. New York: Oxford University Press, 2006.

———. *The Problem of Slavery in the Age of the Revolution, 1770–1823*. Ithaca, N.Y.: Cornell University Press, 1975.

Donald, David Herbert. *Lincoln*. New York: Simon and Schuster, 1995.

Douglass, Frederick. *Narrative of the Life of Frederick Douglass*. From *Slave Narratives*, in *The Library of America*, edited by William L. Andrews and Henry Louis Gates, Jr. New York: Literary Classics of the United States, 2000.

Filler, Louis. *The Crusade Against Slavery, 1830–1860*. New York: Harper & Row, 1960.

Franklin, John Hope. *Runaway Slaves: Rebels on the Plantation*. New York: Oxford University Press, 1999.

Gara, Larry. *The Liberty Line: The Legend of the Underground Railroad*. Lexington: University of Kentucky Press, 1967.

Goldfield, David. *The American Journey: A History of the United States*. Upper Saddle River, N.J.: Pearson Education, 2007.

Green, Constance. *Eli Whitney and the Birth of American Technology*. New York: HarperCollins, 1956.

Havighurst, Walter. *River to the West: Three Centuries of the Ohio*. New York: G. P. Putnam's Sons, 1970.

Hine, Darlene Clark. *The African-American Odyssey*. Upper Saddle River, N.J.: Prentice Hall, 2005.

Horton, James Oliver, and Lois E. Horton. *Slavery and the Making of America*. New York: Oxford University Press, 2005.

Jordan, Winthrop D. "Unthinking Decision: Enslavement of Negroes in America to 1700." In *Interpreting Colonial America: Selected Readings*, edited by James Kirby Martin. New York: Dodd, Mead & Company, 1974.

Larson, Kate Clifford. *Bound for the Promised Land: Harriet Tubman; Portrait of an American Hero*. New York: Ballantine Books, 2004.

Liston, Robert. *Slavery in America: The Heritage of Slavery*. New York: McGraw-Hill, 1972.

McNeese, Tim. *The American Colonies*. St. Louis: Milliken, 2003.

———. *America's Civil War*. St. Louis: Milliken, 2003.

———. *The Ohio River*. Philadelphia: Chelsea House, 2004.

———. *The Rise and Fall of American Slavery: Freedom Denied, Freedom Gained*. Berkeley Heights, N.J.: Enslow Publishers, 2004.

McPherson, James M. *Ordeal by Fire: The Civil War and Reconstruction*. New York: McGraw-Hill, 1992.

Nye, Russel B. *William Lloyd Garrison and the Humanitarian Reformers*. Boston: Little, Brown and Company, 1955.

Pease, William H., and Jane H. Pease, eds. *The Antislavery Argument*. Indianapolis: Bobbs-Merrill, 1965.

Quarles, Benjamin. *Black Abolitionists*. New York: Oxford University Press, 1969.

Sherwin, Oscar. *Prophet of Liberty: The Life and Times of Wendell Phillips*. New York: Bookman Associates, 1958.

Siebert, Wilbur H. *The Underground Railroad*. 1898 Reprint. New York: Arno Press, 1968.

Smedley, R. C. *History of the Underground Railroad*. Lancaster, Pa.: Office of the Journal, 1883.

Stone, Edward, ed. *Incident at Harper's Ferry*. Englewood Cliffs, N.J.: Prentice-Hall, 1956.

Strick, Lisa W. "The Black Presence in the Revolution, 1770–1800." In *Freedom to Freedom*, edited by Mildred Bain and Ervin Lewis. Milwaukee: Purnell Reference Books, 1977.

Strother, Horatio T. *The Underground Railroad in Connecticut.* Middletown, Conn.: Wesleyan University Press, 1962.

Thomas, John L. *The Liberator: William Lloyd Garrison; A Biography.* Boston: Little, Brown and Company, 1963.

Trodd, Zoe, and John Stauffer, eds. *Meteor of War: The John Brown Story.* Maplecrest, N.Y.: Brandywine Press, 2004.

Walters, Ronald G. *American Reformers, 1815–1860.* New York: Hill and Wang, 1978.

Ward, Geoffrey C. *The Civil War: An Illustrated History.* New York: Alfred A. Knopf, 1990.

FURTHER READING

Altman, Linda Jacobs. *Slavery and Abolition in American History*. Berkeley Heights, N.J.: Enslow Publishers, 1999.

Douglass, Frederick, and Michael McCurdy, eds. *Escape From Slavery: The Boyhood of Frederick Douglass in His Own Words*. New York: Alfred A. Knopf, 1993.

Katz, William Loren. *The Westward Movement and Abolitionism, 1815–1850*. Orlando, Fla.: Steck-Vaughn, 1996.

Sterling, Philip, and Rayford Logan. *Four Took Freedom: The Lives of Harriet Tubman, Frederick Douglass, Robert Smalls, and Blanche K. Bruce*. Garden City, N.Y.: Doubleday, 1967.

Streissguth, Thomas. *Slavery*. History Firsthand Series. San Diego: Thomson Gale, 2001.

Tackach, James. *Abolition of American Slavery*. San Diego: Thomson Gale, 2002.

White, Deborah Gray. *Let My People Go: African Americans 1804–1860*. In *The Young Oxford History of African Americans* 4, edited by D. G. and Earl Lewis. New York: Oxford University Press, 1997.

WEB SITES

Aboard the Underground Railroad: A National Register Travel Itinerary
http://www.cr.nps.gov/nr/travel/underground/

Biography of Frederick Douglass
http://www.frederickdouglass.org/douglass_bio.html

Harriet Tubman
http://www.harriettubman.com/

The Underground Railroad
http://www.nationalgeographic.com/railroad/

National Park Service: Underground Railroad
http://www.nps.gov/undergroundrr/

Abolitionism: Judgment Day
http://www.pbs.org/wgbh/aia/part4/4narr2.html

Abolitionism in America
http://rmc.library.cornell.edu/abolitionism/

Social Issues: Abolitionism
http://www.u-s-history.com/pages/h477.html

PICTURE CREDITS

INDEX

137

ABOUT THE AUTHOR

TIM MCNEESE is associate professor of history at York College in York, Nebraska, where he is in his sixteenth year of college instruction. Professor McNeese earned an associate of arts degree from York College, a bachelor of arts in history and political science from Harding University, and a master of arts in history from Missouri State University. A prolific author of books for elementary, middle and high school, and college readers, McNeese has published more than 90 books and educational materials over the past 20 years, on everything from Picasso to landmark Supreme Court decisions. His writing has earned him a citation in the library reference work *Contemporary Authors*. In 2006, McNeese appeared on the History Channel program *Risk Takers/ History Makers: John Wesley Powell and the Grand Canyon.* He was a faculty member at the 2006 Tony Hillerman Mystery Writers Conference in Albuquerque, where he presented on the topic of American Indians of the Southwest. His wife, Beverly, is an assistant professor of English at York College. They have two married children, Noah and Summer, and two grandchildren, Ethan and Adrianna.